Powerful Passive Profits

Disclaimer and Copyright Notification:

Copyright © 2019 by Chris Carpenter

The contents are based on the author's personal experience and research. Your results may vary, and will be based on your individual situation and motivation. There are no guarantees concerning the level of success you may experience. Each individual's success depends on his or her background, dedication, desire and motivation.

NOTE: Some of the recommendations in this report might contain affiliate links. If you click on the link(s) and purchase such a product based on my review and/or recommendation, I will receive a referral commission. Whether I receive a commission or not will not have any effect on the purchase price of the product. Additionally I am sometimes offered a complimentary product to review. My decision to promote these products is based on my own satisfaction with the products. I do not recommend crap, and any review I make will be based on my own experiences, which are not typical. You could do better, you could do worse, you could do nothing at all, and that is totally out of my control.

We make every effort to ensure that we accurately represent our products and services. There is no guarantee that your results will match examples published in this report.

Some links may change or even not work for many reasons beyond the control of the author and distributors. They cannot guarantee or otherwise be responsible for what you might find when you click through to sites not under the control of the publisher of this report.

Table Of Contents

Here's How to Turn Your Dreams into a Reality	1
What Would It Mean For You To Have This In Your Life?	7
Dream A Big Dream	7
Create a Visual Representation of Your Ideal Life	8
Who Do You Admire That Lives This Kind Of Life?	9
Following Highly Successful People Is Great For Your Mindset	9
Capture The Excitement You Feel, Forever	10
Improve Your Mindset	11
Do You Truly Believe You Can Live This Kind Of Life?	12
Manage Your Expectations	14
Everyone Gets Excited When They're Chasing the Dream of Getting Rich	16
This Can Be Your Reality	17
Is It Really Possible For An Income Stream To Be Truly Passive, Forever?	19
Setting Goals and Deadlines for Your Dreams	23
Goals Help You Find True Success	25
Write Your Goals Down Now	25
Create a Roadmap for Your Success	27
Know Exactly What You're Working to Achieve	27
Know What You're Doing before the Start of Each Day	28
Eliminate Uncertainty	29
Remain Flexible	29
Never Be Afraid To Do It Better	30
Examine Your Talents, Skills, Passions, and Interests	31
Choose Your Top Business Models	32
Stacking Passive Income Streams	33
Choose Your Favorite Business Model	35
Don't Let Anything Stand in Your Way	35
Create an Outline of Your Roadmap	36
How Much Time Do You Have Available To Work?	38
Setting Yourself up for Success, Avoiding Burnout, and Finally Following Through	40

Brainstorm What Your Obstacles Might Be 41
Create a Vision Board 42
Tell People about Your Plans with Confidence 43
Surround Yourself with Like-Minded Thinkers 44
Consider a Coach, Mastermind, or Accountability Partner 46
Joining a Mastermind Group 47
Finding an Accountability Partner 47
Keep Your Goals at the Top of Your Mind to Avoid Burnout 48
Create Solid Daily To-Do Lists That Are Easily Managed 49
Don't Reinvent the Wheel Every Time 50
Don't Think of Mistakes as Failures 51
Consider Your Past 52
An Overview of the Passive Income Life 54
When to Add another Passive Income Stream 56
The $5 A Day Model 58
Passive Income Stream Business Builders 59
Consider Your Unifying Theme or Brand 61
Affiliate Marketing Websites 62
Kindle Publishing 63
Blogging 63
Email List Building 64
Product Creation 64
Continuity Programs 65
The Dream… 66
Choosing a Niche 67
Coming Up With Possible Niches 69
Creating Your Brand 71
Ideas for Better Branding 72
Building Up What Works and Ditching What Doesn't 72
The 80/20 Principle 73
Here's How to Build up Each Passive Income Stream 74
Passive Income Stream #1: Affiliate Marketing Websites 75
What Is It? 76
What You Need 79
Technical Needs 80

- Quality Content 80
- Be Patient 81
- Traffic 81
- The Five Steps You Should Take 82
  - Step one: 82
  - Step two: 83
  - Step three: 84
  - Step Four: 85
  - Step Five: 87
- Tying This Together with Other Passive Income Streams 88
- Passive Income Stream #2: Blogging for Passive Income 89
- What You Need 91
- The Five Steps You Should Take 93
  - Step one: 93
  - Step two: 94
  - Step three: 94
  - Step four: 96
  - Step five: 97
- Tying This Together with Other Passive Income Streams 98
- Passive Income Stream #3: Kindle Publishing 100
- What You Need 101
- The Five Steps You Should Take 104
  - Step one: 104
  - Step two: 105
  - Step three: 105
  - Step four: 106
  - Step five: 106
- Tying This Together with Other Passive Income Streams 107
- Passive Income Stream #4: Email List Building 108
- What You Need 111
- The Five Steps You Should Take 115
  - Step one: 115
  - Step two: 116
  - Step three: 117
  - Step four: 117

- Step five: 118
- Tying This Together with Other Passive Income Streams 119
- Passive Income Stream #5: Product Creation..122
  - What You Need 123
  - The Five Steps You Should Take 124
    - Step one: 124
    - Step two: 125
    - Step three: 126
    - Step four: 127
    - Step five: 127
  - Tying This Together with Other Passive Income Streams 128
- Passive Income Stream #6: Continuity Programs 130
  - What You Need 131
  - The Five Steps You Should Take 132
    - Step one: 132
    - Step two: 132
    - Step three: 133
    - Step four: 133
    - Step five: 134
  - Tying This Together with Other Passive Income Streams 135
- Be A Self-Starter For Incredible Passive Income 136
- Tie Your Income Streams Together 138
- Stay on Top of Your Passive Income Streams 140
- Managing Your Income Streams..142

Here's How to Turn Your Dreams into a Reality

How incredible would it be if you could take an entire month off from work and still earn as much as you did the month before? How amazing would it be if you could double or triple your income, at will?

It can certainly feel like that's just a wild dream. The truth is that people are working to achieve that kind of life all the time. It doesn't come easy, of course. The people who've set up lucrative passive income streams for themselves put a lot of blood, sweat, and tears into it – especially in the beginning.

These highly successful people have a mission. They have a mission to develop high-earning, passive income streams so they don't have to actively work every single day of their life. They don't want to have to put in X amount of work each day to earn X amount of money. They want the work they do today to pay off for years to come.

This kind of wealth generally doesn't come from just one income stream, of course. Highly successful people like to stack passive income stream on top of passive income stream so they can earn more with less effort over time. It's a fun and easy decision for them to jumpstart yet another income stream.

It's easy to separate yourself from people like that and think they must be blessed wizards who've been sprinkled with fairy dust. You think they must have a magic wand or secret formula to be able to become wealthy from passive income streams. You sometimes dream it can be you but you don't really believe it.

Yet, there was something that made you want to pick up this book. There was some part of you that believed, even if only for a moment, that it would be possible for you to achieve this kind of life. Maybe you know someone who started from zero but now earns from multiple passive income streams every day. You know they aren't any better or smarter than you so you start to feel like that could be you. (Spoiler alert: it can be).

Perhaps you've read my own success story. I work hard every day in my business and always have, because I enjoy what I do and I want more. Much of my income comes from the multiple passive income streams I've built up over the years.

It wasn't that long ago that I was just like you, working like crazy and feeling like I wasn't getting anywhere. I didn't have passive income streams to speak of at that time. If I didn't get work done on a particular day, I didn't earn money on that particular day. I didn't want to live life like that.

There was a point, again, not too long ago, where I felt like I had to throw in the towel in running my own business altogether, but I can be stubborn and didn't want to give up. I was very deep in debt with seemingly no way out. My offline retail business had me seeking ways to unload inventory and get more business online that could hopefully help get me out of the mess I was under.

One thing led to another and I found out that there was a huge, huge online marketing world I hadn't been aware of before. There were many ways to earn money that I wasn't even aware of at the time. There were ways to earn money from my existing business and many ways to set up totally unrelated passive income streams.

I started following link after link and success story after success story. There were many so-called Internet marketers who were making huge amounts of money... And I mean huge. I couldn't get enough of their stories and I dreamed of being in their position, someday.

I decided that's what I wanted as well and I was determined to get it. I tried strategy after strategy, determined to get those multiple passive income streams going. Unfortunately, it was often hard to focus. I'd try a strategy here and there and nothing was working.

All signs indicated that I should just give up. But, I remained persistent. I didn't want to just give up. I couldn't give up. I was in a position that I needed some major, major wins to get out of debt and get away from the massive load of stress I had.

Finally, I found a strategy that did work and worked in a big way. I took some major chances, including putting additional debt on the credit card, but it really paid off. Finally, I had an income stream that wasn't tied to hour-per-hour, dollar-per-dollar.

That strategy worked, to the tune of multiple tens of thousands of dollars. I was hooked-- I wanted more. This gave me the boost I needed to investigate and take real action with additional income streams.

I continued to set up successful income streams that allowed me to check in on them every now and again as I watched them grow. I tweaked and nurtured these income streams along the way, as I watched my bank account grow.

That, in my opinion, counts as delightfully passive income and I was thrilled. I was able to get out of debt and saw the kind of financial success I'd always dreamed of.

I didn't stop there and can't see myself ever stopping because I enjoy business so much now. I continue to build assets and find new passive income streams so my income can grow higher and higher.

I enjoy that I can't see myself retiring from actively working at existing passive income streams and finding new ones, at least not anytime soon. It's invigorating and fun to develop multiple passive income streams.

Overall, it doesn't feel like "work" because I enjoy what I do. I have up and down days, certainly, and tasks I enjoy more than others, but I can't complain because it's truly a dream come true.

The world doesn't come crashing down if I take a day off. I'm cashing checks and getting money deposited into my accounts all along the way. I'm here to tell you that I'm not any different from you. I'm not smarter than you and the only thing that separates you and I right now is time, know-how, action, and perseverance.

I'm well aware that many reading this have struggled with taking action (or maybe taking consistent action) and not giving up until you've truly achieved your goals. My hope is that things are going to change dramatically for you as a result of having read this book.

There's a reason that little voice told you that it was time to put your effort into creating multiple passive income streams, even if you've tried and failed in the past.

That little voice told you to reach for the sky. There's a reason for that. It's because *this* is your time. I'm going to teach you all the ins and outs of setting up incredible, passive income streams.

Note that I'm not just going to hand you the steps and call it a day. Most of your success depends on your mindset. You haven't failed to create passive income because you don't have the right steps—I'm sure you have many products and books on your hard drive right now that contain perfectly workable passive income stream plans. You need strategy and a mindset that embraces abundance. You need confidence. You need to know that this time, you absolutely are going to succeed. That's why I'm going to spend quite a bit of time helping you with your mindset before we dive into the "do this, then do that" steps.

You can consider this a two-phase process. Improve your mindset and then you can take massive action to create multiple passive income streams.

I can't, of course, promise you a specific income or dollar amount. But, I can promise you that what I'm going to present to you works. Each of these methods can lead to a full time income. When you combine multiple income streams, your bank account can be full to bursting.

You have to push through and never give up, even when the going gets tough. You have to dedicate yourself to the dream of reaching your goals, having an abundance mindset, being able to push through at any cost, and having a Reason Why and passion for doing what you'll be doing. If you have those things, you absolutely can, and most likely will, succeed.

What Would It Mean For You To Have This In Your Life?

Before you can achieve your dream life, you have to know what that looks like. If you had multiple really solid, high-earning passive income streams paying you day and night and you were able to achieve your financial dreams, how would that change your life?

Dream A Big Dream...

It's time to do some brainstorming and dreaming. Brainstorm where you would live and what your home would look like. Maybe you picture yourself in a brand new home with all the bells and whistles. Maybe you have no intention of moving and you picture yourself in your current home, but it's totally paid off.

Picture what you might wear and buy. Picture the numbers in your savings account, checking account, and investment accounts. See your children in your mind's eye as they graduate from a prestigious university that you were able to pay cash for.

See yourself traveling all around the world, getting to live out your dreams and not worrying about the cost at all.

Whatever it is you dream about, picture it. Really get all of your senses involved. Feel the emotions you'll feel when those dreams turn into a reality.

This is a pretty fun exercise, right?

If you craft a life like this in your dreams, it will be much easier for you to believe in yourself and stay motivated until those dreams become a reality.

Create a Visual Representation of Your Ideal Life

You can even go as far as to create a vision board or mind movie. These are visual representations of the things you're working hard to achieve in your life.

You can get poster board or a bulletin board and find images and text that represent the things you want. Put this somewhere prominent where you can look at it in the morning and before you go to bed at night.

Whenever you hit the "wall" and don't feel like you can keep going as you work on these passive income streams, you can look at the vision board you made for yourself so you can get motivated again.

A mind movie is the same thing, by the way— you're just creating a video from something like a PowerPoint presentation that has all the things you're working to achieve. Create it, save it as a movie, put motivational music to it, and watch it often.

Who Do You Admire That Lives This Kind Of Life?

Success leaves clues. Find people you admire who have successfully set up multiple passive income streams. Find people who are happy and who freely share about things they did that helped them get to where they are today.

Following in the footsteps of highly successful people is beneficial in many ways. For one thing, you can avoid making some of the mistakes they made and get to where they are more quickly. If they freely share what they did that worked and didn't work, you can use that information to reach success more easily.

Following Highly Successful People Is Great For Your Mindset

Following highly successful people does wonders for your mindset. It's probably the case that you don't know very many people in your "real" life who've set up successful passive income streams, because most of the people that you know have regular jobs, where they get paid for the hours they work.

Even people who own businesses often have their income tied to how many hours they put in, or how many hours their business is open.

Your family might look at you like you have two heads when you suggest that you're going to do set up an income stream that can continue earning you money long after you put in the hours.

You have to ignore the doubters, including your own nagging internal voice, and seek out people who are on the same path or who have already succeeded. They will help you keep your head on straight when you start to doubt. They will understand that family sometimes doesn't get it (family will start to "get it" when those paychecks start coming in).

Capture The Excitement You Feel, Forever

You dream of earning a great living by setting up multiple passive income streams. You're really excited right now— so pumped up that you just know you're going to succeed.

But, how will you feel a week from now? Will you still feel as excited? I hope you will, but I doubt it. When you move from the dreaming and planning stage to the action-taking stage, strange things start to happen.

You start to wonder why in the world you thought this was even possible. You wonder what you were thinking. You run into roadblocks and you stumble. You start to believe that you can't succeed after all and that you were deluding yourself before.

Improve Your Mindset

Your mind is resisting because you don't have the right mindset yet. You need to work to change your mindset so you can keep going and keep taking action, no matter what.

One of the best ways to do that is to fill your day with success stories. Read books of those who have been successful and that you admire. Join or form a mastermind of very motivated people, who are at your level or slightly above. Read the blogs and archives of successful people you hope to emulate.

You might even consider hiring a coach or a mentor to help you along. Hire someone who will help jumpstart you to action and help keep you there. They'll help you keep going even when you don't feel like it.

It can take big money to hire a coach, and if you can't afford that yet, how about getting an accountability partner? This person can help make sure you follow through with your plans, even when you hit that wall and even when it looks hopeless.

So, figure out who you admire who lives this kind of life. Keep your eye on the prize by seeing that they were able to actually succeed and have achieved the things you want to achieve. This is real and their success proves it.

This opens up your mindset because you'll see that you aren't working for nothing. It is possible and you will follow through and make it happen.

Do You Truly Believe You Can Live This Kind Of Life?

This goes along with what we just talked about in the section above. Do you really, truly believe that you can live this kind of life?

You might say yes, that you do believe.

Okay, so do you believe it enough to follow through with setting up multiple passive income streams, no matter what?

Or, are you going to allow that little voice inside your head tell you that you can't and won't succeed? This negative voice likes to creep in as soon as you start taking massive action.

If you believe strongly enough that you can and will succeed, you can quiet this voice. You can push through anything, even when every ounce of your body feels like giving up.

Your mindset will keep you strong. It's sometimes the only thing that will keep you strong. The crazy thing is that so few people realize just how important mindset is. They buy book after book and strategy after strategy on "fast money" income streams but don't realize that mindset is the biggest part of the battle.

They start taking a little bit of action, but soon they're on to the next Bright Shiny Object.

You've probably had that experience yourself. If you're like many people I work with, then you've bought a lot of "make money" products before. You really want to succeed but you rarely follow through to the end.

You see, mindset can be tricky sometimes. It can cause you to believe that the answer to your hopes and dreams is possible, but that it's still "out there", waiting for you to discover it. I went through that phase for years myself, and only when I sat back and realized that I already knew enough and was good enough to succeed, did my mindset let me quit chasing those bright shiny objects and focus on my existing skills.

That might be the case with you also, so just quiet that negative mindset for a while and take an inventory of your existing skills and abilities before continuing to chase the shiny objects.

I want today to be different for you. I want today to be the day you decide that things are going to change.

I'm going to help you learn how to successfully set up multiple passive income streams. Are you ready to follow through and make it happen or do you just want to continue filling your hard drive with hopes and dreams without ever turning them into a reality?

I'm sure you're ready for the former. You're ready to finally make it happen.

Since that's the case, it's time to follow through with the mindset strategies I'm sharing right here. You're going to take massive action, set solid goals, and stop at nothing. You're going to figure out your overarching Reason Why you want and need these passive income streams.

You aren't going to dismiss this entire section on mindset and skip right to the moneymaking sections. I know that's a very tempting thing to do. But I'm telling you that the "secret sauce" to massive success is having a mindset of abundance.

This is business. This is your life. It's your time to succeed. Get your mindset in the right place so you can eliminate the resistance you feel and push through to your ultimate success.

Manage Your Expectations

Before I go too far into this, I want to tell you that it is 100% possible for you to earn a full time income (many times over) by setting up multiple passive income streams. You can do it. You can change your life. Full stop.

With that said, you have to have the right expectations going in. You have to know that it will be hard. You have to know that you will feel like giving up sometimes.

Are you prepared for that? When that loud, doubting voice sounds in your head, are you going to push through anyway? Are you going to finish projects even if you feel resistant to it?

Professional athletes have to manage their expectations. They have a great goal. They are intrinsically and extrinsically motivated to follow through, no matter what happens.

They push through and make it happen even when they're not feeling well or feel like they can't take a single step forward. That's what you need to do.

Too many people who are in business think they can just do the work and everything will come together. They don't consider the fact that they won't feel like doing the work most of the time. They will try to wait for the "perfect conditions" to work.

Highly successful professional athletes and highly successful business people play and work even when they don't feel like it. They don't wait for optimal conditions to take action. They do it because they have a Reason Why and solid set of goals that pushes them forward even when it seems impossible.

Prepare yourself for the fact that sometimes you'll have to do the work even when you doubt yourself. You have a plan and you need to follow through with that plan.

You'll have to do the work even when conditions aren't perfect. You'll work when you don't feel well, physically and mentally.

You'll do the work no matter what. You'll do the work because you have your eye on a huge prize— financial freedom, forever.

You feel excited right now and you're sure that this is the time you're going to follow through and succeed. You know that all of those other times no longer matter. You're pumped and ready to go.

Everyone Gets Excited When They're Chasing the Dream of Getting Rich

That's a great feeling and I'm so glad you're excited. The thing is, everyone gets excited when they're chasing the dream of getting rich. Everyone gets excited when they know they have a solid plan of action in front of them, like this one.

But, you've gotten excited before. You've had very good plans of action in front of you before. Yet, you haven't achieved your dreams yet. You've floated from one passive business model dream to the next and you don't have anything to show for it.

If you want things to change in a big way, then you have to change your actions in a big way.

You feel excited now and you're ready to tackle these big, huge dreams. You're pumped up.

But, you won't always be. Whether it's tomorrow or next week or next month, there will come a time when you don't feel like you can do it anymore. There will come a time when you feel so resistant that you drop these big plans for good.

You'll drop these big plans and start salivating at the next marketing email you receive that promises you big, easy riches.

Don't do that. Prepare yourself for the fact that you'll feel doubt and resistance on your journey. Prepare yourself for the fact that you'll see marketing messages that will threaten to take you off course.

You're going to have to work for it, and working for it is hard. Work hard on your mindset. Remind yourself of your overall goals every day. Work even when you don't feel like it. Work even when you're not feeling 100% your best.

Don't wait until conditions are perfect to work, because they never will be. Work even when the initial excitement has worn off.

It's the daily consistent action that's going to add up to big things. It's not the next "hit" of a Bright Shiny Object that lands in your inbox.

Are you ready to do the work and follow through no matter what? If you are, you can finally achieve your dreams. You can finally earn passive income that will change your life, forever.

This Can Be Your Reality

There's nothing that sets those highly successful people you admire so much apart from you. Most of them aren't better or smarter than you are.

The only difference is that they had solid goals and an unbreakable roadmap for reaching those goals. They did the work even when they doubted themselves and even when they didn't feel like it.

They pushed through until they were successful and kept on going until their daily success rituals became habit. Daily, consistent action-- that's what you need.

If you can keep your eye on the prize and keep your goals and Reason Why at the top of your mind, you'll soon become one of the people others admire so much. People will soon be studying you, looking for clues for why you're so successful.

Turn this into your reality. Stop at nothing until it is.

Is It Really Possible For An Income Stream To Be Truly Passive, Forever?

Let's talk a little more about what your expectations should be for your passive income streams. Can you really set something up once and benefit from it forever?

No, you can't. Ongoing work and oversight will be required. You'll need to pay attention to changing conditions and learn to adapt when needed.

You'll need to tend to your passive income streams over time. It won't take nearly as much work as it did in the beginning, but the work is still there.

It makes me cringe when I hear that someone has set up an amazing, awesome passive income stream that was really profitable in the beginning and then just let it sit there until the money slowly dwindled away to nothing.

Think of your passive income streams as if they were part of a garden. You do most of the work in the beginning. You tend to the soil, plant the seeds, and water them. They sprout and bloom and produce fruit and you're happy.

If you never tend to that garden again, the plants might still grow for a while. But, they will also be overtaken by weeds and slowly wither away from lack of water and attention. They'll never be high producing and beautiful again and will eventually die out altogether.

If you take just a little bit of time to water your garden when it needs it and to weed it when it needs it, it will grow to be big and beautiful and will produce for many years to come.

It will grow while you're sleeping and while you're away for a few days. It will grow while you're goofing around and doing the things you like to do. It will grow while you're building another garden to double your reward.

But, you have to come back to water it sometimes and pick its rewards so it can grow more. You have to weed it and tend to it and put loving work into it.

It's harder in the beginning, when you're setting the garden up. It's so much easier and so much more passive once it's gotten going. It's so rewarding and so amazing that it does most of its work while you're not even there.

Your passive income streams are exactly the same way. Think of them as a garden that you work hard to set up and return to tend to when needed. If you're away for a few days, no big deal. If you're sleeping, no big deal. If you pay someone else to tend to it a bit while you're whipping around the world, traveling in style, it still grows.

The same is true for your passive income streams. You set it up and do the hard work in the beginning. You tend to it every now and again. You make changes when conditions change. You hire people to do the work you don't like to do. You keep your eye on it and do what you can do to help it grow.

"Set it and forget" it is largely a myth. There are some passive income streams you have to tend to more in the long-term than others. There are others that are pretty much hands off that only need a tiny bit of TLC.

The work you do in the long term can be minimal. These passive income streams can help you enjoy your life so much more.

It really stinks for your only income to come when you're actively working. That's draining and I could never go back to working in a situation where if I didn't work for a particular hour, I wouldn't get paid.

I want to "get paid" even while I'm sleeping and even while I'm on vacation. I want to be able to enjoy life at my beach condo (paid for with my online income streams) and not have to work 24/7.

It's a fantastic life, and I'm excited that you're at the point where you're serious about living it.

Get into the mindset of what a passive income really means. It means you can take a week off or even a month off if you want… but only after the income stream is set up and steadily producing.

Setting up passive income streams means you can travel, spend time with family and friends, and live life on your own terms.

It may not be a "set it and forget it" type of lifestyle, but that doesn't exist anyway. The passive income lifestyle does exist and it's incredible.

Are you ready? I think you are.

Setting Goals and Deadlines for Your Dreams

You're a dreamer, which means you might not be used to stopping and setting goals and deadlines before plowing ahead. You dream these big dreams and you hope to achieve them someday.

You dream big, but how solid are your goals, really?

Maybe you know that you want to live in a bigger, better house with a lot of land, for example. But what, exactly, does that look like? By when do you want to be able to move into your new dream home?

You dream of earning a wonderful, full-time passive income – but what does that really mean? A full-time income to you might be very different from what a full-time income means to the next person.

You can't decide that you want to earn a full-time income and not spell out exactly what that means to you. It's important to set very specific goals that you hope to achieve. This helps put you in a mindset of success and gives you an exact target to reach.

Being specific dramatically improves your chances of actually achieving your goal. That's because there is actually something to achieve! You have to have that target there so your brain can get to work on reaching it.

Not only is it important to set very specific goals, it's also important to put deadlines on those goals. You know that you someday want to earn $10,000 a month in passive income. Do you want to earn that amount per month within 10 years or do you want to earn that amount per month within three months?

Soon, you're going to create a roadmap for yourself based on your goals. The roadmap you would create for a 10-year deadline is extremely different from the roadmap you would create for a three-month deadline.

That's why it's important to be very specific and to put deadlines on your goals. This is an extremely important part of your success. If you aren't specific, then you don't truly have anything to aim for. If you don't set deadlines, then you don't know exactly what work you should be doing, how much of it you should be doing, and when you should be doing it, to achieve your goals.

Don't just dismiss this is as something you don't need to do. You need to think long and hard about your goals, make them as specific as possible, and put deadlines on those goals. Not only that, but you need to write those goals down.

Writing your goals down solidifies them. It makes them more real and tangible. In fact, I suggest you write your goals down over and over again. Many successful people write down their goals every morning or at night before they go to bed, or both.

Revisiting your goals often helps you keep going even when the going gets tough. Revisiting your goals helps you keep an eye on the prize so you can keep going no matter how discouraged you feel at that particular point in time. You have big things you're meant to achieve and that you're going to achieve. Your goals are at the forefront of this achievement.

Goals Help You Find True Success

If you don't set deadlines and goals, you probably won't ever do the work or live up to your full potential.

I know that's a bold statement, maybe shocking to some, but I want to set the tone right away for you. Read that prior sentence again and again until you understand it, and believe in its importance. Otherwise, you'll be stuck chasing bright shiny objects, trying to find the next hit of hope.

You're beyond that now. You're at the point where you're ready to find true success, not just the kind of success that lives in your dreams. Setting goals paves the way for you to choose your business model and find success. Setting goals paves the way for you to set up multiple passive income streams.

Write Your Goals Down Now

Don't just read this section about goals and dismiss it as something you don't need to do or something that you'll do later. In fact, get out a pen and a piece of paper and start brainstorming your goals right now.

Yes, right now. Or, if you prefer, open a fresh word processing document and start typing your goals, but for most people, writing them with pen and paper is a stronger action subconsciously.

Place these goals in a prominent place where you can look at them often. Incorporate these goals into your vision board or mind movie. You should have very specific goals related to your life and business.

Note that your goals might change over time. That's okay and it's to be expected. Keep up with your goals every day and remain flexible.

Make it so that every action you take in your business and in your life puts you one step closer toward your goals.

Slow and steady wins the race. I call this incremental progress. As much as possible, take a step forward every single day. Yes, there will be setbacks, but 2 steps forward for every 1 step backward will still get you to the finish line.

At first, it might seem impossible that you're going to achieve your goals, especially if you've set your sights on the stars. I promise you that it's not impossible at all. Set your goals, and make them very specific, and you'll find success.

Create a Roadmap for Your Success

It's important to plan this out. Successful people plan their own success, down to the smallest detail. You need to plan out what you'll be doing this year, within the next six months, within the next month, within the next week, and day-to-day.

You should never work on your business and not know what you're doing or why you're doing it. Everything you do, down to the smallest detail, has to be in line with your goals and the Reason Why you're working to create multiple streams of passive income.

You have to have your goals and your reason why firmly in your mind. There's a reason I've had you do so much work in figuring out your goals and the overall reason why you want to be successful and earn a great, passive income.

Know Exactly What You're Working to Achieve

There are many reasons why it's important to create a roadmap for your success. Essentially, you're reverse engineering your own success.

You know the endpoint you're working to achieve. Now you just need to figure out how to get from point A to point B. Making an overall plan of which business models you're going to work with and exactly how you'll implement those business models is the best way you can ensure your own success.

Know What You're Doing before the Start of Each Day

You should never wake up and not know what you're doing that day. Remember that you want to take a step forward today (and every day). What will that step forward be today? You should be able to look at your roadmap for success and know what you're doing tomorrow and next week. You should have an overall idea of what you need to have completed over the next six months and over the next year.

One of the biggest reasons why so many people try to be successful and fail is because they are unsure. They flow from one project to the next project without getting anything done at all. They don't know what they're doing each day when they wake up. They're throwing spaghetti noodles against the wall and hoping they stick. They aren't taking steps forward towards their goal destination, towards their Point B.

You're going to take a better approach. You are going to plan out your success very clearly.

You want to make it so easy and break it down so much that a seven-year-old could follow your plan and be successful.

I'm exaggerating, but not by much. This will help you get into the right mindset because there won't be any uncertainty. You'll have a set number of things to get done every day. Every day, you'll be one or more steps closer to financial freedom.

Eliminate Uncertainty

When you don't know exactly what you're supposed to do, that leaves room for uncertainty. You'll start to doubt yourself and your path.

By being very well planned out, you'll avoid this uncertainty and you'll be able to push through, completing projects left and right. You'll be a true action taker. You won't have half unfinished projects all over the place.

By planning well, you won't have to think about the next step as it's happening. Having to think about and doubt every single step is extremely unproductive.

Again, it's important to eliminate uncertainty however and wherever you can.

Remain Flexible

What I'm about to say next might seem a little bit contradictory. While you want to be extremely well planned, you also want to leave some room for flexibility.

Things might change—the landscape of your income stream might change in large or small ways. If your passive income streams are on the Internet, the Internet, websites, or tools might change. Customer and client expectations might change. Competition might change. Opportunities will emerge.

What I'm saying is don't have blinders on, you want to be aware of changes t hat affect what you're working on, and adapt to them.

Never Be Afraid To Do It Better

If you're following in the footsteps of other highly successful people, then you might come across a method of doing something that is way better than the way you'd planned it. Adapt and move forward.

You're new to this, after all. The people who've come before you have figured out all of the mistakes and how to avoid them. They've figured out a way to reach point B from point A much more quickly.

It makes sense, then, to remain flexible even after you've created a really thorough road map. It makes sense to allow yourself to make changes in your roadmap from time to time.

You need to be discerning about what you change. You don't want to let the next bright shiny object throw you off course. However, if you're smart about the changes you make, it can definitely benefit you. Be flexible and make changes when and where you need to.

It's never a bad thing to find better, faster ways of doing something. As long as you're not switching gears before you finish your product, it's a great thing to be flexible.

For example, when I set up my first paid membership site, the available tools were much different than are available now. I found a way to make them work, but if I were doing things over again, I'd use different tools and software. Things would be easier for me. So if you're doing setting up a similar paid membership site, you wouldn't want to follow me exactly, you'd take advantage of today's technology.

But now that I have a successful membership site, should I change it? If you start making progress using today's technology and get almost to your Point B of completion, should you change your plans because a new type of technology appears? I'm thinking probably not.

Examine Your Talents, Skills, Passions, and Interests

There are so many successful and talented people out there that it's easy to be swayed in one direction or another. It's easy to want to follow in their footsteps even if their business model isn't something within your skillset.

It pays to realize that we are all different. It's important to examine your talents, skills, passions, and interests as you develop your roadmap for success and choose your business models.

If you're better at one thing than another thing, then it makes sense to focus on what you're good at. Use your God-given talents, passions, and interests to help you succeed much more quickly.

Examine the available business models. Don't choose something just because it's the "hot" thing to choose. Don't choose something just because it's what other marketers are talking about right now.

Choose something because you know it is the right path for you. Choose something because you're excited about it. Choose something because your talents, skills, passions, and interests are a perfect match for it.

Choose Your Top Business Models

Examine the business models I've detailed for you in this book. Choose a few business models you might want to follow through with. Which ones look extra fun and profitable to you? Your answer is probably different from the next person's answer, and that's just fine because all of the business models have incredible potential.

As a special note – you may have noticed that many of the business models in this book go hand-in-hand. You may have noticed that I am very active in several of these business models myself.

This isn't because I'm unfocused and jump around from business model to business model. It's because each "business model" is nestled within my overall business plan.

I've built my list in my niche because that supports all of my other business models.

The books I release on Kindle are a great way to advertise my other products, build my list, and brand myself as an expert.

My membership site, Earn 1K A Day, is a great way to lead to my other products and services, though I generally give members my products for free. My products also lead people to Earn 1K A Day, of course.

Everything is tied together. Each gives me an incredible passive income stream and they all add up to an amazing income that keeps going even if I take a day off and even if I want to take it easy at the beach condo.

Stacking Passive Income Streams

Once you get to a certain level, it makes sense to add on additional passive income streams that are related to the income streams you've already gotten going.

You'll notice that my efforts are all in the same niche. My goal is to help entrepreneurs achieve their dreams and shape their own financial future. Most of the things I do are within that niche.

People who are interested in my Internet marketing products are most likely interested in my Kindle books. People who join my free Facebook group are probably interested in upgrading to my paid membership site, Earn 1K A Day.

This is not the same thing as being scattered and releasing Kindle books on one topic, creating a membership site within another niche, releasing info products in another niche, and developing multiple niche affiliate sites that are on a completely different topic.

That approach can work and many people have built up nice passive incomes that way. But it's so much less work and so much more profitable to earn within one niche, because once you become known as an authority in one niche, people tend to gravitate to you as an "expert". Each income stream builds on the next. It's the smart way to build up passive income.

If you've found a profitable niche, then I urge you to add additional passive income streams that are related to that same niche. They will all feed off of each other. You will corner your market. Everywhere people in your niche go on the Internet, they will find you and your products. They will find your payment buttons.

Focusing multiple passive income streams within the same niche is definitely a smart plan and I highly recommend it. Consider this tip as you create a roadmap for your success.

You don't want to be so scattered that your Kindle books, products, membership sites, and affiliate sites are totally unrelated. Yes, you can earn a full-time income that way, but you'll be creating so much more work for yourself.

Be focused and totally corner a niche with multiple passive income streams, and you'll have it made.

Choose Your Favorite Business Model

Now that you know that you're not forever married to one particular business model, it's time to choose the one that's calling to you the most. Choose the one that's most in line with your passions and talents.

Maybe you're a writer and you can't wait to start writing books to release on Kindle.

Maybe you have your eye on a niche that buys info products like crazy.

Maybe you love the idea of setting up an authority affiliate site or blog, or mini affiliate sites.

Whatever it is, make it your mission to become obsessed with this business model. You're going to learn more about it, inside and out.

You're going to absorb the information I give to you related to this business model, but you're also going to seek outside information. You're going to study those who are wildly successful with this business model.

Don't Let Anything Stand in Your Way

Note that, no matter how detailed the guide you're following, you're going to have questions along the way if you've never done a certain task. Don't throw in the towel. You have to be a self-starter.

One of the biggest differences between those who succeed and those who do not succeed is that the person with the success mindset won't let anything stop them.

If they have a technical question, they find the answer on Google, or YouTube, or they ask a friend.

If they're feeling stuck and unsure, they find someone to help them. They let absolutely nothing stand in their way.

That's the way you need to be.

Create an Outline of Your Roadmap

Now that you have chosen your business model and you've (hopefully) become obsessed with making it work, you're going to ignore all the other business models.

That's right. The other business models don't matter in the slightest after you've chosen the first one.

They don't matter until the first one is fully up and running and earning for you.

I had you choose a few that you're interested in, but you're going to save those for later.

Right now, you should have tunnel vision about the business model you've chosen. Now, it's time to start creating an outline for your roadmap of success, based on the business model you've chosen.

Note what you already know to make it a success. Note the overall steps you need to take to really get going and start earning with this business model.

From what you know right now; break down the larger projects and steps you need to earn with this business model into tiny, manageable chunks. This is something you'll do after you learn more about your business model.

For now, just know that you don't have to get scared of the larger steps. You can break down every single step so you can easily tackle it.

The point is to make tentative plans for how this business model will help you achieve your goals. You're creating a solid plan for following through with your chosen business model until you start to see an income from it. Then, and only then, will you make plans that include the other business models.

Focus, focus, focus.

Create a 12-month plan for your success (with tentative plans for the business models you will implement after the first one). Write down your goals related to this plan. Which goals will you have reached by next month? Which goals will you have reached within six months? Which goals will you have reached within the next year?

Write down the individual steps that are going to help you achieve those benchmark goals. Break it down for this month, this week, and daily. You should plan yourself so well that you know exactly what you're doing tomorrow.

Start today. There is no reason to put this off. Every day that you work in a concentrated way puts you one step closer to your goals.

How Much Time Do You Have Available To Work?

I want you to know that I fully realize that some people can only work on this part time because you have other obligations. If you really dedicate yourself, you can achieve a full time income fairly quickly, no matter how much time you have available to work.

You might have a full-time job, are a full-time caregiver, or have limited time for other reasons. Some who are reading this are dealing with a chronic illness that makes them feel less than their best every day. If that describes you, please do not throw in the towel. Keep going. It might take you longer than a full-time person, but you still can achieve.

Remember, time will pass anyway, so you might as well be making some progress while it does.

Once you have everything set up, you'll be able to live a life that accommodates your other full-time responsibilities. Having multiple passive income streams will allow you to eliminate stress and worry and have more than enough money, even if you only work part time.

In my opinion, setting up multiple passive income streams is well worth it for those who don't have a lot of time and who are really frazzled with their current lifestyle. This could be the freedom you need.

Setting Yourself up for Success, Avoiding Burnout, and Finally Following Through

You might be wishing that I would get to the moneymaking steps already. The funny part is, this "mindset stuff" you're reading right now is 90% of the "money making stuff."

I can give you the steps for creating multiple passive income streams all day long. The truth is that if you don't have the right mindset, and most don't, then you won't succeed.

I could give you 10 simple steps that would absolutely guarantee you would make $1 million and most people still wouldn't follow through. They would find a reason or an excuse or they'd get swayed by a faster-track method of making $1 million.

Get in the right mindset and the money will follow.

The steps are easy; the mindset is difficult.

This is a major change from what you're used to. But, I hope you're excited about it. I hope you're ready to eliminate your scarcity mindset and get into a mindset that will allow you to create multiple passive income streams.

I've mentioned several times that the early steps and early days are going to be the most difficult. Once you get your passive income stream up and running, it's pretty much smooth sailing. It's getting to that point that can be draining.

It can be so much work that you get burned out and give up altogether. You see the next shiny object and you're off to that because you're so burned out and you're in "puppy love" with the new method because you haven't put the work in yet.

You'll find yourself right back where you started and the cycle will continue.

If you take steps to set yourself up for success, then you can and will avoid burnout. You'll finally be able to follow through and find the success you deserve to find. When you're burned out, it just seems like you can't take another step forward. This is going to help you get past that problem.

Brainstorm What Your Obstacles Might Be

There are going to be things that pop up as you work that really discourage you. There will be obstacles that come along no matter how well planned out you are.

No matter how strong and determined you feel right now in these early stages, these obstacles can really get you down.

Beat these obstacles at their own game by trying to predict what might happen.

Think of all the worst-case scenarios that might knock you down in your weakest state. Maybe you'll get some unexpected bills.

Maybe you'll run into a technical hurdle. Maybe your friends and family members will turn against you and think that what you're doing is stupid.

You know your life and you know what is most likely to stop you. Think about what has stopped you from success in the past. Write it all down and get it all out. Getting it all down on paper makes these potential obstacles much less scary right from the start.

Now, brainstorm ways you can overcome these obstacles. Think of all the things you can do to make these obstacles no problem at all.

Planning ahead for the things that might take you off path or make you quit altogether will make you so much stronger. These obstacles will make you feel weak, but that's okay because you've already planned the solutions.

Now, you can look back on the notes you've taken on your solutions for getting past any obstacle. You'll automatically feel so much stronger. Brainstorming solutions to potential obstacles is a huge, huge thing that can dramatically improve your chances of success.

Create a Vision Board

I know I've already mentioned this, but it warrants another mention. If you haven't already, create a vision board that contains all of your hopes and dreams—the things you're passionate about achieving. Put it in a prominent spot where you can look at it all the time, especially when you're feeling burned out and discouraged.

Fill it full of images of the things you want and the things you're determined to have. Fill it with the results of your hard work – and know that you're going to achieve and get the things you want so badly.

Tell People about Your Plans with Confidence

One of the best ways to ensure that you follow through with your plans is to declare to other people that you're going to do something. Tell your friends and family members what you plan to do, with confidence.

Now, I have to say that some family members and friends are better to tell than others. There may be some people in your life, unfortunately, who are only of the mindset that you have to go to work and punch a clock for an hourly wage, because that's what they do, and their parents did, and all their other friends do. They don't see that there are any other options. They might look at you like you're crazy when you declare your plans.

Don't be disappointed when they look at you like you're crazy – like you're an alien with two heads. Let their discouraging comments go in one ear and out the other. Your dreams are possible and untold numbers of people have successfully set up multiple passive income streams all over the world.

You already know it's possible, now you just have to do it. If someone tells you that you can't do it, just ignore them. Your mindset is strong enough to handle it now.

Focus most of your energy on the friends and family members who will support you, no matter what. Focus your time and energy on those who will cheer you on and even help hold you accountable. Telling those people will be a huge boost and will improve your chances of success. Public declarations of your goals instantly help you get into the "I AM going to do this!" mode.

I hope you have people in your life who are supportive of your dreams. If you don't, or if you need additional support from people who have similar dreams and plans, I urge you to join my free Facebook group, The IM Inside Track. This is an incredibly supportive group of likeminded thinkers (many of whom will have read this very book) and will help you achieve your dreams.

Surround Yourself with Like-Minded Thinkers

This goes hand-in-hand with what I just said above. It will do wonders for your mindset if you communicate with people who are on the same path you're on.

You can find communities of entrepreneurs on Facebook, Skype, forums, and so on. You might be able to find a local Meetup.com group, if you'd like to meet with like-minded thinkers in person.

You're much more likely to achieve if you have a community that cheers you on and sees things in the same way.

Don't surround yourself with people who tell you that you can't do it. Declare your intentions loudly and proudly to those who support you, but start to distance yourself from people who put burrs in your mindset.

Find a community that will help you when you're down. Find a community that will help boost your confidence when you're feeling burned out. Find a community that will help you figure out a way to get past it when you hit the wall.

Ideally, the community you find should have members in it who are at the beginner level, intermediate level, and advanced level. You can support others while others support you.

It will help you if there are people who are newer to this than you are. It gives you a great confidence boost and improves your own follow-through when you're able to pass along your newfound knowledge to others. Simply by reading this book, you'll have more knowledge about developing multiple passive income streams than most people have.

It will help you if there are intermediate level business owners in the group. Those who are at the intermediate level have done so much and are already earning. Whether you're at this level or below, you can learn a lot from the ups and downs of others. You're going through the same thing, which is wonderful because it can help you keep going just to know that you're not alone.

It will help you if there are advanced level business owners in the group. This is what you aspire to. They've gone through it all, have gotten past the wall, and come out the other side. These are the people who didn't let anything stop them. They had a solid Reason Why and solid goals. This is what you aspire to and this is the level you're going to reach.

We learn a lot when we surround ourselves with others who are below us in success and above us in success. Being near successful people lets us know it's possible, even when we're feeling down or stuck. This is so important on a mindset level.

Consider a Coach, Mastermind, or Accountability Partner

In addition to finding a community that that can help you, it can be beneficial to find people you pay to help you even more directly.

Probably at the top of this list is finding a coach. There are business coaches out there who will help you get started and who will help you achieve much more quickly.

Your coach will help with your mindset—and we know that's the biggest part of the battle.

They can even be a little harsh with you when you're letting yourself get stuck. They can push you so you achieve your dreams. They won't you sit back and do nothing. Many people need that kick in the butt every so often.

Your coach can help you avoid mistakes and make even more money. They can teach you from their own experience. They've been on a journey, and what they've learned on that journey is priceless. The right coach can make a dramatic difference in your own journey.

Joining a Mastermind Group

It can also be beneficial to join a mastermind group. Mastermind groups are usually quite small and are filled with business owners who are on a similar path.

As a group, you can share what works and what doesn't, what you're struggling with, what your goals are, and more. You can learn from what each other is going through right now so you can all boost each other to success more quickly.

In some cases, joining or forming a mastermind group can be a great way to find people to partner with on specific projects. That way, you can each dip into your resources, combine those resources, and come out ahead, much more quickly.

Finding an Accountability Partner

It's a wonderful idea to find an accountability partner. Ideally, you should find someone who has similar goals. Find someone who is as much of a go-getter as you are.

This accountability partner should keep up with you and call you out on it when you fall down on the job, and vice versa. You're each other's cheerleader, each making sure the other is staying on track. This experience can be invaluable.

If you're trying to find a like-minded accountability partner, you can ask for one on my free Facebook group, The IM Inside Track, or in my popular high-end membership site, Earn 1K a Day.

It's important to find someone who is a good personality match and who you won't mind communicating with every day. Find someone who will cheer you on but call you out on it when you mess up.

Keep Your Goals at the Top of Your Mind to Avoid Burnout

I don't mean to beat a dead horse, but this is just so important that I can't help but repeat it over and over again. It's important to keep your goals at the top of your mind so you can avoid burnout.

You aren't just waking up to work every day on your passive income streams for no reason. You aren't even just doing it for money. You have very specific goals that are extremely important to you.

The vast majority of people never achieve the goals that are most dear to them. They think they'll get around to it later, but they never actually do. I strongly believe that you're here, reading this right now, because you are meant to be different.

You are going to become part of the small percentage of people who actually work hard and achieve their goals. You are going to develop multiple passive income streams that allow you to achieve every goal on your list.

Review your goals each day as soon as you wake up. Review your goals each night before you go to bed. Even that simple act will help boost your chances of success very dramatically.

Create Solid Daily To-Do Lists That Are Easily Managed

You have your big plan – your roadmap. You have your goals and you're ready to go.

But, you can't wake up in the morning and not have any idea of what you're supposed to be working on very specifically that day. You should be able to wake up and tackle your to-do lists, getting everything done with no thought at all.

Take your roadmap and break it down into a daily to-do list the night before each day.

Creating a to-do list seems like such a simple thing. It seems like such a basic level thing that everyone is doing, right? Yet, do you create a to-do list every day? Are you sure that every item on your to-do list is in line with your goals?

It's time to start writing daily to-do lists the right way. That way, you can just get up each morning and start working without wasting valuable time wondering what your next step should be. Uncertainty kills productivity.

If you have big projects on your roadmap, divide those projects into easy to manage chunks – something you could work on for 15 minutes at a time or 60 minutes at a time on your to-do list. The idea is to fill your to-do list with very easy to manage tasks that won't take forever to complete.

Create checklists for your most common tasks so you don't have to reinvent the wheel each time. The work you do will be better and you'll be sure to follow through since you won't have to think about what the next step should be.

These to-do lists will help you stay on track and will help to ensure that everything you do is in line with your goals.

Don't Reinvent the Wheel Every Time

You're not rowing through uncharted waters here. There were many, many people before you who have developed multiple passive income streams like the ones you're about to set up. The path has already been cleared and this book is giving you a mega-speed boost.

Don't feel like you have to reinvent the wheel. You aren't making this up as you go along. I'm telling you exactly what you need to do. I've also made it clear that it's important to seek the advice of very successful people who've already accomplished what you want to accomplish.

Realize that you don't know what you don't know. You won't know some of the finer details until you take action. But you know the bigger, most important steps because of the successful people who've come before you. You just have to repeat what they've done.

Follow in the footsteps of those who've been successful and you can become successful yourself. It should give you a huge boost to know that these are time-tested strategies and that you don't have to reinvent the wheel.

It should comfort you to know that an incredible number of people have successfully developed multiple passive income streams online and live the life they want to live.

Now it's your turn.

Don't Think of Mistakes as Failures

It's also important that you don't think of your mistakes as failures. We all make mistakes. Even the most successful people in the world make mistakes.

In fact, some of the most successful people in the world have made the *most* mistakes. They've made the most mistakes because they've taken the most action.

It was Wayne Gretzky who said that you miss 100% of the shots you don't take.

Sure, you won't make any mistakes if you don't try. But you also won't succeed.

Start yourself off the right way by realizing that you absolutely will make mistakes and you will have failures. You'll work really hard and things might not take off as quickly as you think they should. You might get frustrated.

But, you're still making progress. You're learning along the way. Every mistake and every failure is one step closer in the right direction.

Don't think of mistakes as failures. Consider them learning opportunities. Learn and move on. It's making you a much more well-rounded success story.

You can absolutely learn from others' mistakes and you should work to avoid making the same mistakes they have. You don't want to make mistakes you could have easily avoided and others have definitely made this a smoother path for you.

Still, mistakes will happen and you should embrace them. Use mistakes as fuel for your fire instead of a damper.

Consider Your Past

Consider your past efforts to make more money by starting your own business—online or off. Have you been determined to set up passive income streams before? Have you ever actually followed through and found success?

The chances are good that you made some mistakes and would do things differently this time around—especially if you gave up. Hopefully, you now have a much better mindset and know that you can and will succeed.

Embrace your past. Don't feel like a failure. Don't kick yourself time and time again for past mistakes. Pat yourself on the back because you've dusted yourself and you're trying again.

You just have to make sure that this time is different. Make sure you follow through and take massive action for massive paydays—you have a much better chance this time around. You now have solid goals and you have a Reason Why. You've also managed your expectations. Not only that, but you're following in the footsteps of success.

You know, without a doubt, that this time is going to be different. The people who've already found success aren't any different or better than you are. The only thing that's different is that they pushed through to the end. That's it.

We all get the same 24 hours in a day. From this point on, you're going to use your 24 hours in a much different and better way. Every 24 hours, you're going to take several steps closer to your goal. Nothing is going to throw you off track. If you veer off track slightly at any point, you're just going to right your course, dust yourself off, and keep on going.

An Overview of the Passive Income Life

Get ready – because you are about to live the life of your dreams. That isn't just marketing speak. That's me being very excited for you because everything you've ever dreamed of is about to come true.

It's not because because a genie has appeared to grant all of your wishes, or you've found a magical pushbutton solution, or even because of this book. It's because you're finally in a place where you're ready and where you're not going to let anything stop you.

You've already dreamed of the life that having passive income streams can afford you. You can live where you want, do what you want, have enough money for extras, finance your children's education, give money to charity, volunteer your time, and so on. You can travel around the world, not work at all while you're traveling, and still make money. You can take days off when you're sick and still make money. You can have power go off during a bad storm and still make money.

Earning passive income is phenomenal and life-changing. Each passive income plan is different. There are some that require more work than others. There are some that might be more lucrative for you than others. There are some that you're better suited to than others. There are some things they have in common, of course. You can and should interlink them for even more earning power.

You'll work hard to set up the passive income stream in the beginning. I'm going to give you an overview of the work involved. The amount of time you'll spend setting things set up depends greatly on your current level of experience, your mindset, your follow-through, and the amount of time you have available to spend on this task.

You're going to have the roadmap you created for yourself, and you're going to use any mistakes you make as learning opportunities. You'll examine those who are already successful and do everything you can to copy their success.

No matter which passive income stream you've chosen, you'll work it until you see results. You won't stop until you see results. You know people have been successful with that passive income stream before, and there's nothing different about you.

You'll closely examine your results and you'll know exactly what is working and what isn't working. You'll scale up what is working so you can earn better and faster. You'll cut out what isn't working. You'll remain flexible.

Then, you'll scale up what is working even more. You'll push that passive income stream until you're squeezing every last drop of income from it.

Once you get things going, you can start to outsource. Not only will your income stream work for you on autopilot, but you can have outsourced workers take care of some of the finer details. That four-hour workweek lifestyle you might dream of living is well within your reach at this point.

You'll also learn to invest in your business. Some people want to set their business up totally for free, even after they're making money. It's definitely possible to get started for little to nothing, depending on the business model you choose. However, you should also be aware that you'll be so much more successful if you invest in your business and yourself.

It's foolish not to put some of your profits back into your business. This will help you scale it up. Your money will start to multiply itself. This is how a smart business operates. You're not just playing at this – this is not just a hobby – this is a true business.

You're going to push it until you succeed. You're going to push past any walls that have erected themselves in your path.

You'll add other passive income streams only when you're ready and only when that first income stream is mostly working on autopilot.

When to Add another Passive Income Stream

This book is all about creating multiple passive income streams. If you think you can just jump in and try to work all of these income streams at one time, you have another think coming!

It's important to get one passive income stream up and running before you move on to another one. You need the first one to be earning for you before you should even consider another one.

If you work a little on this project and a little on that project and then a little on yet another project, without finishing any of them, you're going to get overwhelmed. You're also going to delay your success.

In this, as in all business, focus is everything.

I definitely understand the feeling that you want to work on everything at one time because you think it's going to help you achieve more quickly. It just doesn't work like that. Finish one thing and then move on to the next thing.

Many people think they should set up multiple passive income streams at the same time because they see successful marketers and business people doing that. You see me releasing books on Kindle, releasing new info products, running my membership site, and so on.

Why is it okay for me to have these multiple passive income streams with many different projects going at once, but not you? It's because I fully focus on one at a time. My info product business is already up and running and successful. My membership site is already up and running and successful. The same goes for each of my passive income streams.

But when I first conceived of and started my membership site, I totally focused on that for quite a while, got it running successfully and bringing in new paid members on a regular basis, before I started working on something new.

It's important to finish what you start. Finish at least one successfully earning project per passive income stream before you consider another one. Note—sometimes there is overlap.

You might need to set up a website to host your squeeze page. I'm talking about where you put your focus. The overlap is a good thing for when you are ready to fully focus on an additional income stream.

The $5 A Day Model

The first book I was recognized for and the book I'm proudest of, was 5 Bucks A Day. At its heart, it's really about the same thing I'm sharing in this book. It's about getting into the right mindset. It's about choosing one project at a time that you can start and follow through with so you can stack your income.

In 5 Bucks A Day, your goal is to earn just $5 a day from each mini income stream you choose to set up. Once you have one set up, you work on another. You keep on going like that, stacking your income streams to achieve your financial goals.

You can definitely follow this model in combination with the information I'm sharing with you in this book. It depends on your goals and your scale. If you want to stack $5 a day incomes on top of one another, then you can work to finish one quicker project before starting another $5 a day passively earning project.

The importance isn't the number of projects you complete within each income stream or even how much money you're able to make passively with each income stream. The importance is your follow-through. Do you complete projects that help you learn money? Or, do you bounce around like crazy, not finishing anything at all?

That's the question you need to answer for yourself. If you haven't followed through on anything yet (whether you're working for $5 passively a day or $100 passively a day), then you need to work to correct it.

If you have big goals, then make sure each passive income stream you set up connects and builds upon the ones you've already set up. Soon enough, you'll have a huge web of high earning buy buttons and finished projects out there. You'll be able to succeed with your passive income streams.

It's all about moving forward and not looking back. Never, ever, skip around to different business models or projects until you have followed at least one project or full passive income stream through to completion.

Passive Income Stream Business Builders

No matter which passive income stream you choose, you'll be selling something. You're be setting up buy buttons on the web. You're creating ways for people to pay you. People in your niche should (eventually) run into your buy buttons all over the place, in many different ways, and for many different things. That's how you have massive, passive success.

How many buy buttons do you have up right now? If you're frustrated because you've been trying to earn money with your businesses for a while but you haven't had success yet, really think long and hard about this answer. This is a forehead smacking moment for many people.

Do you actually have buy buttons active and ways and reasons for people to pay you online at this moment? Many, many wanna-be entrepreneurs do not – even people who've been trying to run online businesses for years. That's something you have to correct.

With these passive income builders, you'll be using the web to help you sell. I didn't exclude offline methods because they don't work or because you shouldn't pay attention to them. There are an incredible number of ways to develop passive income streams offline. There are also ways to combine offline passive income streams with online passive income streams.

For the purposes of this book, though, I'm going to focus on online-only income streams because they are most accessible to the highest number of people and helping people with online income streams is my specialty.

With these passive income streams, you're going to set up a system where your sales pages and buy buttons on the web will be selling for you 24 hours a day, seven days a week. Your buy buttons and opportunities will be active on the web, whether you are actively present to "sell" or not. Once you get them up, these buy buttons and income earners will earn for you whether you're on vacation or whether you're deep into your next project.

You're going to stack and combine successful passive income streams over time. For example, you can start blogging about a lucrative topic you enjoy. You'll gain an audience and start advertising on your blog, and your blog posts will earn for you for many years to come, one after the other. Once you have that passive income stream up and earning, you can write books related to your niche to publish on Kindle or in an info-product market.

You can also build a highly profitable email list via your blog and via your Kindle books and set up a complete sales funnel for those who sign up for your list. You can fill your autoresponder account with email messages that sell to your subscribers for you, 24 hours a day, 7 days a week.

The combination of things you can do is endless. Remember – you want to set up passive income streams over time that make it so that people can't research or read in your niche without running into your name, your products, your buy buttons, and your content.

You want to be present on your own blog, on social media, on Kindle and other e-book platforms, and in marketplaces in your niche. If you do this, and get a lot of buy buttons on the web, you will have the income of your dreams. Start small and work your way up.

Consider Your Unifying Theme or Brand

It's all about having a unifying theme or brand so it all ties together—that's the smartest way to build up passive income streams.

You *can* choose to be in different niches for each passive income stream (blogging about one thing, creating niche affiliate sites about something else, building an email list funnel on a different topic, and publishing on yet a different topic). Everything builds on everything else.

Both choices are valid in that you can make full-time money doing many things in many different niches as long as you follow through with each thing. But, you will probably earn much more quickly if you set up passive income business builders within a brand or topic marketed to the same audience, across channels.

Next, I'm going to reveal the passive income business streams I'll cover in this book. Pay attention to your initial feeling when I get to each income stream. If your heart pings and you get excited when you read about a specific one, you may want to immediately put all of your focus on that passive income stream. Your gut is telling you something!

Affiliate Marketing Websites

Affiliate marketing websites are an old standby when it comes to ways to develop passive income streams online. There are tons of people out there who research items they want to buy-- their passions, their hobbies, and their problems.

The goal is to create an awesomely informative website that features and reviews products you're an affiliate for, or contains ads of another form, that helps or entertains people.

You'll have buy buttons and opt-in forms on your site to make sales and get people on your list (where you can market to them further).

Kindle Publishing

Ebook publishing certainly isn't limited to kindle, but it is by far the most popular platform. Amazon makes it easy for you to self publish your book – books that are anywhere from a few thousand words long to hundreds of thousands of words long.

Ideally, you'll choose a lucrative, underserved niche with active and enthusiastic readers and release a vast catalog of published works.

Amazon has a great marketing funnel, so once you jumpstart things by getting reviews and early sales, you can start to dominate Kindle sales for your niche. It takes elbow grease in the beginning and you do typically need to release many books before you gain traction.

Blogging

Blogging goes hand-in-hand with affiliate marketing websites—though affiliate marketing websites tend to be more static while a blog is up to the minute.

With a blog, you can be a little bit more personable and really develop a following. The best blogs in all niches have an active and engaged audience who leave comments, subscribe to your updates, and put a lot of stock into what the blogger says.

As a blogger, you'll earn with ads, product recommendations and reviews, list building, and more.

Email List Building

List marketing is one of the most lucrative ways to make money passively on the Internet. You can offer value to people in your niche in exchange for their email address. People will sign up to your list to receive something for free, learn more about a topic, and so on.

You'll recommend things you know they'll enjoy; including products you are an affiliate for and your own books and products. This can be a great passive income stream because you can write autoresponder emails that are sent out on autopilot no matter when someone subscribes. You could be on vacation and people would still be getting your marketing emails.

Product Creation

Creating your own information products to release on the web can be very lucrative. These products can include readable material and e-books, videos, audio, software and more. These products are usually geared toward those who are desperate for a solution of some kind—and your product provides the exact solution they're looking for.

There are many niches out there where people are looking for answers and are desperate for solutions to their problems. If you can create info products that help them solve problems, such as this one, then you can earn a lot of money.

You can have affiliates out there promoting your info products to their audience. They'll email their lists and advertise your product because they're getting a cut of the sales price as a commission. You can make money on autopilot while your affiliates are doing the heavy promotional work.

If you hook up the sales of your products to an email-marketing list, you can market to your buyers again and again. You already know they're interested in what you have to sell because they are proven buyers. This is easy to do with certain affiliate management and products sales solutions on the web (JVZoo is one example).

Continuity Programs

Continuity programs are very smart passive income streams. These are generally membership sites or programs people sign up for. They are charged automatically every month in exchange for whatever it is you've promised them. My own paid a membership site, Earn 1K A Day, has been very lucrative for me.

This is great because it ensures people aren't just buying from you one time. You only have to close the sale once and the payments automatically come out of their bank or PayPal account. This is one of the best passive income streams, though you do have to provide a lot of value each month or people will cancel.

The Dream…

The dream is that you could go on vacation and make sales via your email list autoresponder, affiliate links on your blog, Kindle book sales, sales of your products, and rebills on your membership site… even if you're gone a whole month. You want to set it up so that you can earn a full time income on autopilot.

Yes, you will have to be active and tend to these income streams. But, all of these models can earn for you on their own after you have set them up, without your active hour-for-hour input. These income streams are your 24/7 salesperson. These multiple income streams can change your life.

You just have to stick with it, one at a time. Get one thing going, then another.

There are so many different income streams out there beyond what I've included here in this book. If you have one in mind that you know is workable and has many real success stories attached to it, then by all means go after it.

We'll focus on the common ones I've listed here because they are 100% achievable for you. Go through and choose the one that is the best fit for you to start with. Then, you can scale up and stack income streams to your heart's content.

Choosing a Niche

Throughout this book, you've heard me talking about choosing a lucrative niche. You've heard me say that you can stack income streams in the same niche to boost your effort all the way around. But, what is a niche and how do you find a lucrative one in the first place?

A niche is simply an area of a market of people who are all interested in the same topic. I'm in the Internet marketing niche. You can further break that down by saying that I'm in the Internet marketing mindset and success niche.

A wide niche would be Internet marketing in general, or something like fitness, weight loss, and so on. It's difficult to do well as a new marketer in a wide niche simply because there's so much competition.

Since you're a marketer who wants to make money, you should target a group of people who actively spend a lot of money on a particular topic, interest, hobby, or need.

Key phrase: Focus on people who spend a lot of money.

You shouldn't choose a niche that is popular but where people don't spend money. I don't care how popular it is or how much recognition you can get, if it's not a niche where people spend money, then you won't make any money.

If you want to earn a lot, then you need to seek out a niche that spends a lot.

The sub-niches of the Internet marketing niche are extremely profitable. People are willing to spend a lot and tend to buy many different products that will help them become more successful.

I provide my buyers with products and mindset information that work, so people buy from me again and again.

That's the kind of niche you want to find. You have to put out quality information that works and that stands apart from what the competition is doing.

Internet marketing may or may not be for you. That's just one example-- there are a ton of other very specific, high-spending niches out there. For example, weight loss for new moms. Or certain topics related to golf. Or the self-help and mindset niche. Or dating and relationships.

I can't list all of the possible niches here because that would be impossible. There are so many different niches and sub-niches out there.

Some niches overlap significantly with others. For instance, the Internet marketing success and self-help and mindset niche overlap a lot.

Do the work to find a niche that will pay you well and that you are passionate about. You're going to be working a lot in this niche, so you have to really enjoy it and feel passionate about the people in the niche.

Coming Up With Possible Niches

There are many different ways to come up with niche topics. One of the best ways is to reverse engineer hot-selling niches. Visit the best-selling categories on Amazon, particularly in the book section. Check out which magazines are selling well in the magazine section and which topics they are talking about.

Browse sites like ClickBank.com for popular info-product based niches. Visit sites like AllTop.com that spells out what's hot right now in the blogging and news world. Look at the Google ads that show up when you search for topics related to what you're interested in—this is great for product based affiliate website research.

One big piece of advice I have for you is to make sure that there are some high-ticket items selling well in the niche you're interested in. If the hot-sellers are all $5 ebooks, then you might (eventually and slowly but surely) be able to earn a full-time income, but it probably won't be huge money.

If you focus on a niche where people are actively purchasing high ticket items, the sky is the limit as far as your income is concerned. Do your research and see what's hot and selling to find a niche that will serve you well.

It might be the case that you already know which niche you would like to focus on. Please just make sure it will be lucrative for you. Don't start working in your niche until you're sure of that.

If you still have no idea which niche you should focus on, do some additional niche research. Find those hot niches. Find other online marketers who are already successful and figure out their niche strategy. Look at their blogs and websites. See how active their audience is on social media.

One great litmus test these days is whether a particular niche has a lot of groups and pages dedicated to it, that each have a lot of likes and members.

It's also a good sign if there are ads for low-priced products and high- products in your niche and the signs indicate that they sell well.

See if you can break the niche you're interested in down into smaller parts. If you can target a smaller segment of the niche at first, it might be easier for you to break in and dominate that niche. You can branch out in the niche from there, once you've started to become profitable and have gained an audience.

I could go on for days about niche research. It's actually a pretty exciting topic because the possibilities are endless and the Internet freely gives you all the tools you need to find a lucrative niche.

Settle on your niche before moving on. Then, you can use the business models I give you here to enter into that niche.

You can write Kindle books on topics related to your niche. You can write a blog related to your niche. You can build a list in your niche. You can create info products related to your niche. You can create a membership site in your niche. Each one can build upon the other.

Choose the first passive income stream you're interested in, research your niche, and go from there.

Creating Your Brand

It might be helpful to brand yourself as you enter into a niche and set up passive income streams. When people think of your niche, you want them to think of you.

I've branded myself as the 5 Buck Guy, because of my original 5 Bucks a Day ebook.

Across everything I do in my niche, people find my brand. People have identified with this brand and me because I am down to earth and highly accessible to them, no matter whether they are at the beginner or advanced levels. That's my brand and it means a lot to me to be able to help people.

What is your brand and what does it mean to you? Take a look at how other successful marketers have branded themselves in your niche. You don't want to copy what they do, but you do want to emulate the steps they have taken to become known in their niche.

Ideas for Better Branding

Branding is about consistency, no matter which passive income stream you're focused on at the time.

For example, you can use a similar picture of yourself across platforms. You can use a signature or saying that brands you across platforms.

What is your online persona? How do you want people to perceive you? That all goes into your branding. It's something you should consider as you set up these multiple income streams.

You shouldn't portray yourself as something you're not, but you should definitely let your personality shine through. You don't want to be another faceless, nameless marketer. You want to be someone people know they can trust.

Building Up What Works and Ditching What Doesn't

As you get started with these passive income streams, you're going to find that some of your efforts produce frustratingly little in terms of results.

You're going to find that some of your efforts will produce crazy awesome results that go beyond your wildest dreams.

Part of becoming very successful is knowing what works and what doesn't. If something isn't working, you have to cut it loose.

I won't beat around the bush – it can be difficult to organize yourself when you have multiple passive income streams – even after you've really gotten them going. That's why you have to know what works and what doesn't.

The 80/20 Principle

The Pareto principle (of which I am a huge fan) tells us that 20% of our efforts lead to 80% of our results. That means that many of the things you're doing every day in your business are a waste of time. Many of the things you're doing are necessary but shouldn't get the focus they're getting.

You can get so much more done and earn so much more if you spend more of your time and effort on what is working and getting results. You have to figure out what that is, of course.

Every once in a while, you have to look at the things you're doing. Closely examine your daily efforts and what is working and what is not. Figure out which activities lead to the most income for you.

Scale up the things that lead to most of your results. Ditch the things you're doing that are just a waste of time. Consider outsourcing the tasks that are necessary but don't have the most importance.

If you're ready to lighten your workload and scale up your passive income, then you need to cut the fluff and ditch what isn't working. Work like crazy on the things that lead to the most income for you. In the future, you can outsource those other necessary but lower producing tasks. Soon enough, you'll have passive income streams that produce like crazy and leave you much more time to enjoy your life.

Here's How to Build up Each Passive Income Stream

Next, I'm going to give you specific ways you can build passive income streams. Each of these business models can be adjusted to fit your needs.

The steps I give you offer a path to success. Keep in mind that you need to make the steps your own. Break the steps down into their smaller parts and put them on your to-do list.

Do yourself a favor and set yourself up for success by putting deadlines on each of the steps you need to succeed with a particular business model.

If you'd like to have a Kindle book (or 5) published within the next month, reverse engineer what you need to make that happen. Break the steps down and put them on your to-do list. That's just one example – do that with anything you need to do it with.

Don't forget the mindset stuff I covered in the first half of this book. That "stuff" is what you need to be able to follow through. Once you have the right mindset, you'll able to work through the steps and succeed.

Passive Income Stream #1: Affiliate Marketing Websites

Affiliate marketing websites can be a fantastic passive income stream. Before we go too far into the details, I want you to be very aware of what this is and isn't.

In the past, many people simply set up affiliate websites that offered little value. They focused almost totally on getting search engines to rank them highly for their keywords. They didn't care about the reader and the buyer at all.

I will admit that this strategy worked really well in the past. However, search engines, and people, have come a long way since then. Bad, keyword-stuffed content, is a no-no.

Search engines and people demand value. They won't buy if the goal of your website is strictly to sell to them. They want value. They want to come away feeling like you care about them. They want a touch of personality in your content and in your recommendations. They want something from you that they can't find elsewhere. Google and other search engines try aggressively to eliminate cookie-cutter, no value added, affiliate sites from their search results.

With that said, creating affiliate websites can be fun and they can be fantastic passive income if you over-deliver on value and think about what the reader wants and what's going to convince them to click through your link to buy.

What Is It?

An affiliate marketing website is essentially a site on a niche topic. It differs from a blog in that it generally contains static content rather than blog content. In reality, it's a very thin line and you can call it whatever you want.

One method is to create many sites that focus on a very specific topic. These affiliate marketing mini sites are quick to create and can do well because they serve a particular need. However, you generally need many of them to make any income to speak of. They honestly don't work anywhere as well or as easily as they used to (because of search engine changes). Mini sites are the "throw the spaghetti against the wall to see what sticks" approach.

I suggest you focus on creating an authority affiliate site instead. Over time, you'll add high-quality content, product reviews, and great information people can easily look through when they want to learn something new or are looking for opinions on an idea or product.

You've guessed it – creating an affiliate marketing website is all about the content. People have to feel good enough about your content so they'll go ahead and join your email list or click through your link to the product you're an affiliate for.

You'll make money by adding affiliate links wherever it's warranted – in both text and picture form. Some articles might be affiliate-link free and others might contain a few of them. Browse popular sites in your niche to see how others monetize their sites.

It's all about the readers so you're definitely not going to fill your site with tons of affiliate links everywhere. You'll do a lot better if you keep your readers at the top of your mind. Make product recommendations whenever it's appropriate and really build a reputation with your audience for being someone they can trust.

You want your content to be so good that Google and other search engines want to rank you highly for hot keywords in your niche. You'll hope to rank for specific products and other keywords where people are at the end of the buying cycle – they're ready to buy but just need one push over the edge. That's what your content is going to provide.

Affiliate sites can be fun to build and you can create multiple sites in the same niche, just focus on the most lucrative areas. These sites can be pretty set it and forget it once you have a lot of content on them.

If you have multiple sites, focus a lot on the ones that produce a lot of income for you. You can sell off the ones that are lower producing so you have time to scale up the ones that are producing.

I suggest that you create an email opt-in form for your website— give people something free that they would otherwise pay for so they sign up. You should have your opt-in form visible on every page of your website. Affiliate sites can become awesome list builders.

In fact, you can do really well with a site even if you don't put affiliate links on it at all. Focus on funneling readers to your opt-in form. Place an opt-in form in your sidebar, at the bottom of each article, and in a pop-up.

You can then send people relationship-building content and product offers via email. You'll have their captive attention when you recommend products through your email autoresponder. You might also rank better in the search engines because you won't have affiliate links all over the place (which can lower search engine rankings).

Think about the websites you regularly visit online. Consider which sites you view as an authority and what they do differently from the rest. You can instantly tell when someone only has the goal of selling to you. You can also tell when someone really knows what they're talking about and when they really care about you as a reader and buyer. That's the kind of feeling you want people to have when they visit your website.

This is a slow and steady wins the race kind of thing. You can't build a website today and expect it to take off like crazy tomorrow. You can't expect to make sales right away. In fact, many affiliate marketers recommend leaving all affiliate links off of your website for a month or so until you've built up some authority. This can help with search engine rankings and trust. No matter what you do, focus on quality content and the people who are reading your site first.

Your site will start to gain traction as you have more content. It will be awesome to see that passive income start coming in, building up more each month as you nurture your site. A great authority site can be a full time income on its own. As can a network of mini sites.

What You Need

You need a great niche to be successful with your own affiliate marketing website. Make sure the niche you choose will be highly profitable and that it's a good match for you to be a part of in the long term.

As a side note, there are many site owners who focus on trend marketing. They create sites that capitalize on hot trends. Then, they move on to the next big thing.

Trend marketing is a short-term strategy when you base entire websites about those trends, but they can bring you money. If your focus is on passive income for the long term, then I highly recommend you stick with an evergreen niche. You can always incorporate trend marketing for your niche with fresh content on an evergreen site.

You can focus on a niche like making money, fitness, parenting, relationships, or anything you'd like. But, you really have to dig deep. Find a niche within a niche that you can dominate. What are some sub-niches of parenting, making money online, fitness, and relationships?

Make sure people are spending money in that niche. That's huge and I can't say it often enough. Don't waste your time on a dud of a niche. Stand in front of the money. Focus on active and frequent buyers.

Technical Needs

On the technical side, you need a domain name and hosting. Make sure you choose a domain name that people in your niche will want to click on when they see it in the search results. It's important to build up trust among your audience and your domain name, believe it or not, can help you do that.

You need a hosting company that you can trust. Hostgator is very popular, but it's certainly not the only option out there.

Quality Content

One of the most important parts of running a successful affiliate niche website is writing quality content. You can't just write up drivel and expect it to do well. You can't just outsource articles to a non-English speaker for $1 and put them up on your website and expect it to do well. Focus on quality over quantity – though quantity certainly helps as well and will come with time. A quantity of quality content is the best strategy.

Be Patient

You also have to have patience. It takes time to rank with a new website. But, if you put the effort in upfront, then a website absolutely can be an awesome passive income earner for you.

Traffic

As far as traffic is concerned, you'll definitely want to focus on search engine optimization. This is a different game than has been in the past, of course. Now, it's all about quality and community. It also helps if you build an active social media following. Try to interact on other niche sites and hang out where people in your niche hang out. You're building a brand and a name for yourself.

Don't scare yourself away from paid traffic, though I highly recommend you create a squeeze page on your website that you direct all paid traffic to. You can then capture email addresses to communicate with readers many times over instead of directing them to a single page on your site and losing them forever as they click away. It's much easier to sell to someone on your email list than it is to make a cold sale through a page on your website.

If you focus on creating a site of authority that really helps people, it will last for the long haul. Many people have created full-time passive incomes from high-quality websites like this.

The Five Steps You Should Take

Now, let's talk about the five steps you should take to be successful with this passive income stream.

Remember to make this plan and your site your own. Figure out your goals and exactly what you need to do to achieve your goals with this income stream.

Create a calendar for yourself where you list everything you're supposed to do on a particular day to make this happen.

Step one:

First, choose a niche. Choose a niche that spends a lot of money and that you care about.

You'll be spending a lot of time in this niche, so you have to make sure you'll like it and can develop a passion for it, if you don't have one already.

Since you want to earn a great income, don't just choose something you like – choose something you're sure can be profitable. A profitable niche is one that is very active and that people are spending money on – in both small and large amounts.

Examine similar sites within the same niche. Figure out what has made certain sites successful and others not as successful.

Create a site plan based on your research. Include what you want on your site, how your site is going to stand out from others out there, and even include specific ideas for content.

Step two:

Next, it's time to figure out the technical details. You need to secure hosting and a domain name.

Hostgator is very popular for hosting accounts because they are relatively inexpensive.

Many people use Namecheap for their domain names because they have a solid reputation.

The truth is that there are many options out there, so just choose the hosting account and domain name provider you feel comfortable with.

Your domain name should be highly related to the niche you have chosen. If you've already settled on your brand, and you should have, you may want to make sure it relates to your brand somehow.

After you have your domain name and hosting account, it's time to get your site set up. Even though it's blogging software, I highly recommend you consider WordPress. You can make WordPress look like a static website. Or, as we'll discuss, you can combine the affiliate site method with the affiliate blogging method – it really is a very thin line between the two.

Step three:

Next, you'll want to get ideas for content. You need great content no matter what kind of site you have. Some of your content will be evergreen and some will be "more of the moment." Figure out which topics are most important to your audience and make plans to write about them.

You can set Google Alerts for terms related to your topic. You can browse other popular sites to see what people are talking about. You can also browse forums and question-and-answer sites (like Yahoo answers) for ideas of what to write about.

Pay attention to what people are saying and what they feel is missing from the niche. Get them on your side with great content and great interaction and they'll be much more likely to click your links and buy.

You can also get content ideas by doing keyword research. If you sign up for Google Adwords, you can use their keyword research tool to search for general terms related to your niche—the tool will give you a list of specific terms and relative search counts. You don't necessarily have to run paid ads as a result of setting up this account, but their keyword tool is very good.

I suggest you start out with ideas for 10 different articles you can write for your website. Make your starting content evergreen so it will make sense now and five years down the road.

Now, go ahead and write your content. Inject your personality into it and make sure it stands out from the content of other sites.

Also, make sure you get up the standard site content, such as an about page, a disclaimer page, a privacy policy page, and so on.

Step Four:

Next, it's time to get traffic. People tend to want to be able to just build a site and expect that people will flock to it in droves. "If you build it, they will come." It doesn't usually work that way.

As your site grows with more content and activity, you absolutely will get traffic on autopilot. But, you'll likely have to give yourself a major nudge in the beginning. You have to let people know that your site exists. You have to let Google and other search engines know that your site is worth ranking. That means having excellent content along with working to get noticed.

You can pay for ads to jumpstart your traffic, such as with Facebook ads or Google Adwords ads. Remember to direct people to a squeeze page (a place where you entice people to opt in to your email list by giving them something for free). That way, you capture the traffic forever (or until they unsubscribe) instead of losing them after the first visit.

You can also get traffic by establishing a following on social media. You might consider creating a Facebook page or Facebook group dedicated to your topic. If there are already groups related to your topic, you can join those groups. Share information where you can and make yourself known.

If you're creating a Facebook page, make sure you name it something enticing related to your niche. You can then comment on other popular pages as your page—you'll capture the attention of people who are interested in your niche.

Running a great page, group or profile on social media can help you become known as an authority. It will be much easier for you to get traffic if you start to interact with others in your niche. They'll want to visit time and time again.

You can also pay attention to search engine optimization to get traffic—this is the golden ticket. Do keyword research and find keywords that are often search for, that are related to your niche. Write great content that is related to these keywords. Don't stuff your content with keywords, but use them in your title and where it makes sense to in the body of your content.

You can also do things like creating YouTube videos or running a podcast to get traffic.

Remember, quality is the first consideration, but quantity of articles, blog posts, Youtube videos, podcast episodes, etc. will make you known as an authority. You want to be seen everywhere that your potential customer is likely to go.

Pay attention to what the most popular figures in your niche are doing and make an effort to do something every day that will help you get more traffic. Your links, authority, exposure, and traffic will build up over time—it's a snowball effect.

Step Five:

Now it's time to monetize. Do this once your site is up and running and providing great value to the people of your niche. Find products you know your site visitors will be interested in. These can be physical products or digital products.

As an example, you can become an affiliate for Amazon.com to sell physical products. Amazon affiliates can link to any page on Amazon to earn a commission. They have a full suite of affiliate tools that makes it easy for you.

You can also become an affiliate for digital products through sites like ClickBank.com, Nanacast.com, Zaxaa.com, and JVZoo.com. These affiliate networks mostly host info products.

For certain niches, this is the way to go. For other niches, you'll want to focus on physical products. To make your decision, think about your audience and which products other successful marketers are advertising in the niche. Which products are the people of your niche chatting about on social media?

Remember to focus on building a list from your authority website. This is the most Google-proof way to always guarantee you'll have traffic and people buying through your links. You can send out information and product recommendations to your list at any time. List building is its own passive income stream, but it is the #1 thing you should incorporate into any other passive income stream you set up.

If you choose to start creating your own info products as an additional passive income stream, you can also advertise them on your website and through your list. There are many different ways to monetize your authority website.

Make a plan and stick to it. Focus on what the people of your niche really need and want.

Tying This Together with Other Passive Income Streams

When you're earning and ready, you might consider tying this passive income stream with another passive income stream. Note that the only thing I don't recommend you wait on is building a list—do that from day one no matter which passive income builder you target first. It might not be your focus at first, but it should be set up and ready.

Your affiliate website can become a great hub for all of your other passive-earning activities. You can easily combine list building, blogging, your own info products, Kindle books, and more.

In fact, I highly recommend that even if you don't start with this income stream that you come back to it later on – no matter which income stream you choose. It pays off to have a hub or website of your own.

It really helps for people in your niche to have a place where they can go to learn more about you. This can be a place where your brand and your mission are made clear. This can be a place where you build your list and really make a splash in your niche.

Passive Income Stream #2: Blogging for Passive Income

I've included blogging next because it is so closely related to the passive income method we just talked about. In fact, your authority affiliate website can and should contain a blog. People expect you to have a blog these days. Blogging has become an important part of both online and offline businesses.

A blog is a place where you can share your frequent updates and thoughts. It's where you can share your opinions about news, trends, ideas, and more. You can curate content from other blogs, offer product reviews, and talk about whatever's on your mind that your audience would be interested in.

Readers often take more ownership of blogs they frequent than they do with static websites that offer little in the way of interaction. On blogs, there are typically places where they can comment and leave their thoughts. Blogs, when done well, can quickly become places your audience calls home. This is a great thing for your income.

If you started out with a regular, static website, you can easily add a blogging component. In some cases, the difference between a regular website and the blog is just splitting hairs.

You can use your blog to grow your list. Many successful bloggers include an opt-in form at the bottom of each of their posts. It's an awesome spot because people have just read your content to the end—they obviously like what you have to say! It makes sense to make it easy for them to sign up so they can hear more from you.

Successful bloggers also often have an exit pop-up or an entrance pop-up where they further entice blog readers to join their list. There's generally some kind of on-the-money freebie offered that's hard for the reader to pass up. The money is in the list – keep that in mind no matter which passive income stream you choose. So again, while list building isn't your focus for this income stream, it's a no-brainer to add opt-in forms and take advantage of the fact that blog readers will sign up for your list if you make it easy and enticing.

There are so many different things you can do with your blog. You can use it as a great list builder. You can use it to advertise the sale of your own products. You can even share your progress with your blog readers—keep them interested and active before you launch your product and they'll be a lot more likely to buy on launch day. You can also use your blog to promote products as an affiliate, sell ad space, and more.

Remember that community is one of the most important things with blogs. You want to give people in your niche a place to call home. You want reading your blog to become part of their daily schedule. Take a look at some of the most popular blogs in your niche and you'll likely see that they do a good job with the community aspect.

Blogs mix well with social media and search engine traffic. Google loves to see social traffic on your blog and mentions of it on social sites. Think of frequent updates, a lot of interaction, and a ton of content over time—that's the formula for blogging success.

If you truly want to become an authority and build up a passive income stream, then blogging might be the best passive business model for you.

How is it passive when you're supposed to update so frequently? Remember that this is something you'll build up over time. Once it's up and going, you can outsource some posting, accept guest blog posts, and more. You can also write content in advance and schedule it to release over time.

Blogging does require more care and attention than some of the other business models, but it's a fantastic asset and really a great piece of the passive income puzzle.

Passive incomes from the fact that posts that you wrote in the past, and monetized well, will sometimes rank well in the search engines, so people will find them and click on links. As you build up your total number of posts, there will be more opportunities for readers to find you, not just your new posts, but your old ones also.

What You Need

To create a successful blog, you'll need to start by choosing a niche. Find a niche that is wide enough that you will never run out of content ideas but narrow enough that you can easily stand out and start getting traffic quickly.

Remember that blogs are typically updated frequently – in some cases, they are updated several times a day. Whether you update your blog once a day, a few times a week, or several times a day, you need to make sure that you won't run out of ideas today or five years from now.

Once you have chosen your niche and examined other successful blogs in your niche for ideas, it's time to come up with your domain name. Make it something catchy – something people in your niche will really appreciate. Don't focus so much on creating a keyword filled domain. Focus more on something people in your niche will really respond to.

You'll also need to acquire hosting, if you haven't already, and install blogging software. WordPress is really the preferred way to go these days. Most hosting companies make installation easy with easy script install buttons in your cPanel.

In addition to the technical details, you'll need a steady stream of content ideas. Get alerts about the latest goings-on in your niche. Look for forums and other blogs related to your niche. Stay on top of the latest news and information and keep a log of all the ideas you have. You never want to get to a point where you don't know what to write about.

The Five Steps You Should Take

Step one:

Start with the niche research. Many people want to skip over this step, but you know how important it is. You have to know that the niche you enter will be one that produces money for you. You also have to make sure it has an active and engaged audience. Ideally, you'll find a niche or sub-niche with relatively low competition so you can almost instantly make a splash in it.

Study other successful blogs to get your own ideas. Take note of what you do and don't like. Subscribe to other people's blogs so you can keep up with what they're talking about. Comment in their comments section and interact with their readers. This is a great way to become known as an authority in your niche. It also pays to get to know the popular bloggers in your niche.

Consider the community aspect when you do your niche research. You have to love the community and really want to help the people of that community.

Your blog should be a place where they can go to get the latest information and feel like they belong. You're going to try to earn money from this community, of course, so you have to enjoy the topic and know the things you recommend to them are things that can actually help them.

It's ideal if you can combine your passion for helping people with making amazing passive income.

Step two:

Next, think about the technical details of getting your blog up and running. You need hosting, of course. Again, Hostgator is a good option, though there are many others out there.

Now, go ahead and set up your domain name. Choose something that is catchy and that will really resonate with your audience. If you need help connecting your domain name with your hosting account, or any other technical steps, search YouTube – you can find tutorial videos for just about anything there. Don't shy away from the technical steps just because you haven't done them before.

Step three:

Now, it's time to decide what you're going to write about. Set a goal in your mind to get 30 days of content scheduled in your blog. This content should be helpful, informative, and interesting to read.

People in your niche will expect your content to reflect your personality. People will subscribe to your blog and visit it regularly not only because of the great content you share, but because they want to hear your opinion and read information through your voice.

Comment on topics and ideas you get from other blogs—link to them. Don't be afraid to take a controversial or different opinion than many of the other bloggers take. Subscribe to Google Alerts or another alerts service so you can read the latest information and share your opinion on it.

Blogging software like WordPress allows you to schedule content ahead of time. Get enough content in there for the next month, so content is always being released even when you take a day or a weekend off.

It also helps with momentum-- many people are excited about their new blog in the beginning but quickly lose interest because they weren't getting immediate sales and readers. You know that it can take some time for your passive income stream to build up. Solve the problem of wanting to quit by setting yourself up for success from the start.

Get 30 days of content in there and then write new content as often as you'd like, based on news and ideas that pop into your head along the way. When you're a blogger, the more content, the better. You want to build up so much great content that people will visit regularly. You want them to become addicted to refreshing your blog or checking your RSS feed to see if you've written anything new.

If you're ever stuck, look to other popular blogs in your niche for idea. Whether you're not sure what to write about, or how to engage your audience, or what you should promote. Follow in the footsteps of success. Never copy; just get inspired.

Step four:

It's no fun writing to an audience that isn't there. It's time to get eyeballs on your blog. Thankfully, there are an incredible number of ways to drive traffic.

Since you'll be writing so much content, a lot of your traffic will probably come from search engines like Google. Search engines like frequently released content and that's exactly what you're offering. As you build up your content, your content will rank in the search engines more and more. People will find you because you have so much content out there.

Social media also goes hand-in-hand with blogging. Set up a related Facebook page where you can get fans interested in your topic and funnel them to your blog. Start a Twitter feed and interact with other bloggers and the people of your niche.

It can also help if you write guest posts on popular blogs. You'll get the benefit of capturing their audience. Their audience will get to know you and will hopefully click over to check on your site. Comment on popular blogs. Look for every opportunity to tap into the traffic popular blogs are already getting.

You can also pay for traffic but it's not necessarily something I'd focus on for a blog (it's better for a product offer or list building). If you do end up paying for traffic, I highly suggest you send your traffic to a squeeze page on your blog rather than to something like a blog post or the front page of your blog. The reason is that you want to capture their email address for the long term and not just for the short time they are reading the one post you paid to link them to.

Give them something for free so they will sign up. Then, send an email every time you add a new blog post or whenever you send a very important blog post. Your hope is that you get them addicted to your content.

Step five:

Once you've gotten things going, it's time to start monetizing your blog. You may or may not want to do this right away. Many people suggest that you hold off on putting any form of monetization on your blog until you start to gain search engine favor and people start visiting on a regular basis. It won't matter in the long term, but it's something to consider.

You can start by advertising highly related products you're an affiliate for on the sidebar of your blog. You can write product reviews and include text and image links right within your blog posts to entice people to click through and buy. Your readers have come to trust you—so share your honest opinions about the things you're linking them to.

The best and probably fastest way to build up a full-time income from your blog is to include an opt-in form at the bottom of each post, on the sidebar of your blog, and on a squeeze page (or several targeted squeeze pages). Do everything you can to direct people to opt in to your list by giving them something really great for free. Once they're on your list, you can send them informative emails, entice them to buy things you recommend, and direct people to the new blog posts you write.

Tying This Together with Other Passive Income Streams

Blogging is a great way to start because it really does lend itself well to the other income streams. Your blog can have static website components that are evergreen. It can be a great tool for list building. It can be an awesome way to talk up a new product you're launching, and so on.

Even though it has so much potential, blogging can quickly become exhausting. That's why I recommend you schedule content while you're so pumped up about it. It can take a while to build up but it can be very worth it once it has.

I highly recommend that you incorporate list building into with your blog. I've already mentioned that you should put opt-in forms on your blog posts, sidebars, and squeeze pages to get readers to join your list. You can tell list subscribers about new posts you write, products you recommend, and your own products.

You can use your blog to talk about the new books you plan to release on Kindle. Give away some review copies to get early reviews on Kindle—you can make it a contest on your blog to get people excited. You can link back to your blog in your Kindle books Everything links together and every passive income stream builds the others up, too!

If you create info products, you can talk about your progress on your blog. This helps to get people excited about what's to come and can dramatically improve your sales on release day. Your audience will get really excited and will jump on the product as soon as it's released.

You might also consider creating a membership site your blog readers will be interested in. Perhaps they can upgrade to a paid forum, group coaching of some kind, or even premium articles. This may or may not fly with your audience, so do some testing.

Passive Income Stream #3: Kindle Publishing

Kindle publishing is a fantastic passive income stream. Amazon Kindle has incredible power and has dominated the ebook scene and will continue to do so for the foreseeable future.

Gone are the days when there were gatekeepers telling you that you couldn't publish your book. Gone are the days when editors would turn you down even if what you wanted to publish was quite good.

Amazon makes it easy for you to write a book and publish it to put in front of their audience. If your book proves itself, Amazon's algorithms will do a lot to help you gain an audience beyond the one you already have.

I want to make it clear that you are very unlikely to earn a full-time income with just one book. It is much more likely that you'll earn a great income if you release many books over time – each one netting you a certain amount of money per month, which adds up to a nice amount across your catalog. Some of your books will prove to be higher earners than others. Your books in combination can provide you with the passive income you dream about.

When you release a book on Amazon, you'll need to get reviews from your own audience. You'll need to work to get that initial boost in recognition so you have to work to get some of your own sales to start with. You'll have to push your books yourself, at first, but then it can really take off. Amazon rewards success with much more success.

What You Need

To be successful with Kindle publishing, you first need to research profitable niche ideas. You can't just assume you can come up with a topic, read a book about it, publish it on Amazon, and have it be successful.

I know, there are people marketing courses that say that you can succeed with Kindle by slapping together short books with substandard content, and create a great income stream by doing it enough times in enough categories.

Trust me, though a book or two might succeed, much like with an infinite number of monkeys sitting at an infinite number of typewriters, one of them will create the entire works of Shakespeare. So while it's theoretically possible to hit gold now and then, that won't work reliably enough to bank on it.

Instead, you first have to make sure there's space for your book and that it will actually sell.

I suggest you target niches or topics where the most popular books are ranking under 10,000 or so. With Amazon Kindle, the lower the Amazon rank, the better.

Make sure there's space for you in that niche. Ideally, you want to find yourself ranking within the top 20 after you release. You'll push your book to your own audience so you can get your ranking to under 20,000—leading to a pretty good monthly income for that book. It's much better if your ranking is under 10,000 or under 5,000—then it becomes a phenomenal monthly income for that book.

Do great niche research before you commit to a topic—examine the top 20 books in a category. The top few should be ranking well—under 10,000 or so.

Now examine the bottom few books of that top 20 in your category. You want them to actually not be ranking as well so your book can easily sneak into the top 20.

Pay attention to Amazon's search box when you are researching niches. It will suggest keywords to you. Play around with this until you find a niche or keyword that's popular, but that has room for you to rank well with your own book.

Once you find a great niche, it's time to write a book. If you're short on time but full of ideas, you can outsource. Provide great content that fills a need and you will do well. You don't have to be the next Ernest Hemingway. You just have to write content that will help people and that reads well. Write in a conversational, informative tone and don't be afraid to make your personality shine.

Once you've written your book and its ready for release, you might want to get a team in place that will read your book and review it on Amazon. You can ask other people in your audience. You can even ask friends. It's best if you get people who are active and interested in your niche. Authors call this a "street team."

Try to encourage people to get their reviews up as soon as your book launches. If your book doesn't have reviews, then buyers might not give it a second glance. Books with reviews get clicked on and purchased more. Some who have tested also believe that having reviews on your books gives them a bit of an Amazon algorithm jump.

Just remember that you can't give anything away in exchange for a review except the book itself. There are many authors out there who break this rule. However, you want to follow the rule because you don't want to risk your Amazon KDP account.

Once your book is up and has reviews and is making sales, it's time to rinse and repeat. You won't become rich with just one book or even with 10 books.

This can be a great, passive income stream for you, but you have to release a steady stream of content so you can gain traction. If your books have great reviews and you're releasing on a continuous basis, your sales should snowball from there.

Make sure you're building a list from within the front matter and back matter of your books. One trick is to put an enticing freebie offer within the first 10% of your book—that way even non-buyers who are just browsing the look-inside on Amazon can sign up.

You can then email this list whenever you release a new book. Your sales should snowball as you get more subscribers you can notify.

If you focus on building a list of readers who are interested in your niche and on getting reviews, your sales should really take off over time as long as you keep releasing new content.

Releasing books for Kindle certainly isn't a "one and done" sort of deal. You have to work to gain traction. This is a business model that will snowball over time. It's a fantastic passive income stream because the books you release now will pay off for you for many, many years to come. Your published books will earn for you and your family just as the published works of authors has done for centuries.

The Five Steps You Should Take

Step one:

First, you have to research your topic. Again, make sure the top books within that topic are ranking pretty well – under 10,000 in Amazon sales rank. The bottom few should have a worse ranking so your book can sneak into the top 20 of that niche or category. If the bottom few books in the top 20 are ranking at 50,000+, then there's room for you to get into the top 20.

Search through Amazon's Kindle categories and sub-categories for ideas. Search for keywords in Amazon's search box that you're considering. Do the work of choosing a great niche you can easily sneak into before writing your book, and you'll have much more success in getting sales and ranking well within your category.

Step two:

Now, it's time to research content for your book. Browse through the top books on Amazon related to the book you want to write. Look at their table of contents (using the Look Inside feature) and see what they've written about. Look through their 5-star reviews and their 1-star reviews – what does the audience like and what do they dislike? This can help you come up with ideas for your own book.

Create an outline for your book based on what you find on Amazon (never copy another author's ideas—just get inspired). Brainstorm your own ideas. Browse through related niche forums, sites like Yahoo Answers, and popular niche blogs to see what people in this niche really need and want to know.

Make sure your outline is very detailed—so much so that you don't get hung up at all while you're writing the book.

Step three:

It's time to write your book. Make sure your book stands out and is full of your personality. Make sure it serves a need that is not already served within the niche and with other Kindle books on Amazon.

As you go to publish your book, pay attention to your front and back matter. You should be concentrating on building a list so your Amazon Kindle sales can snowball.

Step four:

Get a review team in place. Make sure people read your book and give their honest review on Amazon. Many authors call this a street team. It's a team they can turn to whenever they need to launch a book with reviews. This team also helps the author spread the word.

Brainstorm ways you can advertise your book wherever and however you can. At the top of your focus should be building a list of people who like to read books on your topic and who actively buy them. Build this list so that you can email them whenever you have a new release.

Soon enough, you'll have enough early buyers and early reviewers that other Amazon Kindle readers will buy your books like crazy. Don't get discouraged if it doesn't happen right away—it takes time to build up but can then become an amazing passive income.

Step five:

Now, it's time to go ahead and write your *next* book. Don't stop at just one because that will not lead to a successful passive income. You need a large catalog of books if you want a passive income.

Indeed, most of your books are not going to bring in a massive income every month by themselves. But, in combination, they will bring in a great income.

Tying This Together with Other Passive Income Streams

This strategy works really well in combination with other passive income streams. Your Kindle books can be a great way to build your list, for instance. Having a list helps you sell Kindle books. Having Kindle books helps you build a list. It all goes hand in hand.

Your info products can be cross-marketed with your Kindle books and vice versa. You can release books on Kindle and then link them to products that contain more personal help and goodies, bonuses, worksheets, and more.

You can advertise your books on your blog or website. Having books published on Kindle gives you massive credibility for things like seminars and coaching. Publishing does wonders for your brand. Even though it's incredibly easy to self publish these days, people continue to be extremely impressed by it.

Passive Income Stream #4: Email List Building

The money is in the list. I've repeated that a few times throughout this book, but it's so important and it's so true. No matter what you do and how many passive income streams you set up, make sure you're building a list along the way.

This list is yours forever. Facebook and Google might come and go, or they might stick around. Do you want to bet your business on it? Of course not.

You can future proof your business by focusing on building your own list of emails. Build a list of emails in your niche and you can contact them when you want, for whatever reason you want (paying attention to email marketing rules and what's best for your subscribers, of course!). If you have a list, then you can have almost instant success with the other passive income streams listed in this book. In my opinion, list building is the ultimate passive income stream.

Every business needs a list. It doesn't matter if the business is mainly offline or online. You need a way to contact your customers and readers whenever you need or want to. A list allows you to build a relationship with the people in your audience. You'll get to know them and they'll get to know you.

People on your list will be a lot more likely to buy from you, click on your links, and sing your praises around the web. People buy from those they know, like, and trust. If they're on your email list, they'll be a lot more likely to know, like, and trust you.

I recommend that you focus on list building no matter which passive income stream you choose. However, I want you to know that you can focus on list building as its own passive income stream. Even if you don't want to run a blog, release your own info products, or release books on Kindle, you can run a successful, profitable autoresponder list that runs for you on autopilot after you get it set up.

The first part of this is setting up a squeeze page. This squeeze page is designed with the sole purpose of getting people to sign up for your newsletter and/or list. Autoresponder companies like GetResponse even allow you to use their servers to host your squeeze page.

You have to entice people to join your list. They aren't going to join your list just because they feel like it or because you want them to. Generally, you have to give them something for free—something so awesome that they would actually pay for it if you had a buy button there.

There has to be a reason they're enticed to hand over their email address and join your list. You might create a freebie product they'll salivate over. If you don't want to create a freebie yourself, you could even buy resell rights or private label rights to something your audience would want, as long as those rights allow you to give whatever it is away for free.

Once you have a squeeze page that sings the praises of the freebie you're giving away (and makes it sound so good people couldn't possibly pass it up), it's time to drive traffic to that page.

When people sign up, they'll confirm their opt-in and receive a link to download their freebie. You now have their email on your list. From there, you can send them additional content they'll enjoy—informative emails as well as sales emails. You can email them with your own offers and with offers you're an affiliate for. Pay attention to what will make the people on your list happy.

You can even upsell people on your list to things like personal coaching or continuity programs. You can advertise lower end products, like info-products and ebooks, as well the higher-end products.

The chances are good that you're on email lists that do just that. Take a look at the people you tend to buy from the most. How do they word the emails that get you clicking and buying? What is it about them that sets them apart from other marketers? Pay especially close attention to those who have enticed you to buy a higher end item. What was it that made you feel okay with spending that amount?

If you study the most successful email marketers, you can take their cues to become a successful email marketer yourself, in your own niche.

This can, of course, tie into your other passive income streams. List building goes with absolutely everything you do as a marketer online. At the same time, you can choose to focus on this building first and only rather than waiting for your list to grow by other means.

If you have a list, then you can't help but be successful. You can set up profitable, relationship building emails through your autoresponder service for the months and years to come. This is about as hands-off and lucrative as it gets.

What You Need

One of the most important pieces of the list-building puzzle is having a reliable autoresponder company. The autoresponder company you choose will help you maintain your list (or lists), create opt-in forms, and deliver your autoresponder emails.

You will have to pay your autoresponder company monthly, but is well worth it. Many of the autoresponder companies work on a sliding scale. It's very inexpensive when you have few subscribers and the price only increases when you have more.

Yes, I know. There are scripts that you can install on your own server that will enable you to host your own list, saving the monthly charges. I did that once upon a time, and it was one of the biggest mistakes I ever made. The reliable autoresponder companies like Aweber and GetResponse work hard maintain a good rating with ISP's, so that their servers aren't flagged for sending spam, thus causing them to get blacklisted.

If you send emails from your own server, and especially if you're on a shared server with other unknown people, the chances of eventually having your server's IP address blacklisted is very likely.

Aweber and GetResponse are two of the most popular options for online marketers. Take a look at what they have to offer and see which one you think will suit your needs. Truthfully, they are probably about equal when it comes to value and service.

Once you've secured your autoresponder account, it's time to create a squeeze page on your website. If you don't want to set the squeeze page up on your own website, then you might be able to use your autoresponder service. For instance, GetResponse generally allows you to set up a squeeze page on their server. You'll probably want to put your squeeze page on your own website however, even if your autoresponder company offers the service. This gives you more control.

Visit the squeeze pages of marketers you admire. If you're not sure what a squeeze page is – it's simply a page that has the sole focus of getting people to sign up for your list. You'll use a headline that captures their attention, a few bullet points that spell out the amazing benefits of the free gift you're offering them, and some call to action text to get them to enter their email and hit submit.

You can use GetResponse or Aweber to create enticing opt-in forms that you can put on your squeeze page. Again, if you're unsure of the technical steps at any point, you can search the help area of your chosen autoresponder company or search YouTube for screenshot tutorials. Don't let the technical stuff stand in your way—there's always a way to get the answer.

It's important that you have something very enticing to give away for free. This might be a free report or free product of some kind. You want something so enticing that people would otherwise pay for it.

Take some time to develop your freebie. Make it something so good that people won't want to pass it up. Then, write enticing copy that will make them want to sign up for your list so they can get it for free.

Don't be so smug as to think people will sign up for your list just for the heck of it without a freebie or some other kind of incentive. People belong to a lot of lists these days and many are tired of getting marketing emails in their inbox.

You can break through the noise and clutter by offering something really great and then sending emails that people will actually want to open. Focus on the relationship and the person at the other end of the screen and you'll do well.

You also have to consider how you're going to advertise your squeeze page. People aren't going to visit it just because you've set it up. Focus on driving traffic to your squeeze page.

You can run paid ads to your squeeze page, using Google Adwords or other networks. You can also link to your squeeze page via social media and other means. Wherever you're online, make sure you're advertising your squeeze page.

Also, in addition to ensuring your freebie is ready to go, make sure you have some great autoresponder copy lined up. Set this up ahead of time so it delivers the first email in a series to people who signed up, on autopilot. Your autoresponder emails should inform and help people while building relationships and making sales.

People differ in opinion as to how many marketing emails you should send in a row. I like to send some relationship building emails and some marketing emails—a mixture. And even when I'm selling, I like to have value there.

You'll find what works for you. What you might do is send one informative email, the next email that's informative but does a soft sell, and the next email that is a more direct, hard sell.

Then, rinse and repeat.

Also, especially if you're driving paid traffic, you may want to upsell people to something paid after they've opted in to get their freebie. People are in the mode where they may be more receptive to buying from you right after they've signed up for your list.

Some marketers like to do a low-priced upsell first. If the person takes the low-priced upsell, they then upsell to something higher ticket.

If you pay for traffic, this can be a nice way to break even or even make money while building your list at the same time. The lifetime value of everyone who signs up for your list is extraordinary.

Treat your list members right at every turn. Test and tweak and find what works for you as an email marketer.

The Five Steps You Should Take

Step one:

First, you have to choose your niche and look at successful opt-in pages for inspiration. Take a look on marketing blogs right now for ideas—many of the best tend to link to a good squeeze page.

Consider the niche you'd like to enter. Are the other list marketers in this niche popular and successful? If you find a relatively popular niche you can easily sneak into, email marketing is as good as gold.

Choose a niche where people are actively spending money and are buying low-ticket items and high-ticket items. Figure out how you can break through with your unique angle and personality, offering something that no one else is offering.

Subscribe to an autoresponder service like Aweber or GetResponse. Read through their help materials so you can get a handle on how to use everything they offer. They have a vested interest in you succeeding with their program and software so they provide a lot of helpful materials.

Design your funnel after you've decided what you're doing. Figure out what your freebie is going to be, what your squeeze page will look like, and what your early autoresponder messages will include.

Find, buy a license to, or create the freebie to give away. This stage is all about planning and understanding.

Step two:

Now it's time to get the tech part done. Get your squeeze page written and set up with your opt-in form. Make sure you have your freebie ready and loaded to be delivered as soon as people sign up for your list. You can include it as an email attachment, upload it to your server, or use a service like Amazon's S3 for delivery.

Try to get at least 7 autoresponder messages (a week's worth or more, depending on your spacing) set up to be delivered after someone has opted in to your list.

These 7 autoresponder messages should help build the relationship between you and your subscribers. I suggest that you welcome an open dialogue with those who subscribe. Invite them to respond to you and reply back when they write you. You aren't just trying to sell within these initial autoresponder messages, though it's absolutely fine to do some selling. Just be sure you have something they will be interested in and are likely to buy.

One good technique, if you're interested in creating future products to sell within your niche, is to ask people to reply to you telling you what their major challenges are in your niche. Then you can take those thoughts and make sure that your future products cover the answers.

Step three:

Now it's time to get traffic. It helps to become known in your niche. One of the best ways to do that is to interact on social media.

You can also make blogging and search engine optimization part of your strategy to get traffic and get people to sign up for your list.

The fastest way to get traffic and to get people to sign up for your list is to pay for ads. Paying for ads lets you instantly know whether your squeeze page is converting or not. This can help you make tweaks so you can get more people to sign up. Then, you can focus on more organic methods of getting traffic.

Step four:

After you've started driving traffic to your squeeze page, it's time to make some tweaks to things like your headline, opt-in button, bullet points, and so on to get the highest possible conversions.

Test one thing at a time and see what works for you. Remember that you can't draw any conclusions until you've gotten significant traffic to your sales page. Try to aim for conversions of over 30%. If you're not getting that after some traffic has rolled in (hundreds and thousands of visitors), tweak to make things better.

Keep on giving and keep on selling. People will sign up for your list for a reason. Don't worry about sending them emails that sell – whether they are broadcast emails or autoresponder emails.

Broadcast emails are those you send out and they go to everyone at the same time. This is great for time sensitive offers and specials. Autoresponder emails go out at set intervals, depending on when someone signed up.

Step five:

Now that you have your squeeze page up and running and you're getting email signups, it's time to get more autoresponder emails locked and loaded.

You might decide to get enough emails ready so you can send a message every three days for a year, on autopilot. This is in addition to any broadcast emails you may want to send. This is great, hands-off income—the very best kind of passive income there is.

Keep building relationships and advertising. Don't be afraid to present affiliate links and buy buttons for your own products. People trust you and they already buy products related to your niche anyway. They may as well buy it through you.

If you want to succeed, then you should set a goal for how big you want your list to be. If you have a list with 10,000 people on it, you should be able to make a fantastic income.

But I know people with a much smaller list that are doing very well (for example, my good friend Connie Ragen Green was earning over 6 figures annually when her list was less than 700 subscribers, and has written a book about her methods (search for her author name on Amazon if you're interested)), and I know people with much larger lists that don't do very well at all. It all depends on the relationship you build with your list.

What is your goal? How much would you like to earn every month from your list?

Keep putting additional squeeze pages and offers out there. Put opt-in forms everywhere you can for everything you do online. Build your list over time and make it a focus and you absolutely can have a fantastic passive income.

Tying This Together with Other Passive Income Streams

As I mentioned, you can focus on list building on its own. You can set up a squeeze page with a freebie offer and drive traffic to the squeeze page to get people to sign up. You really don't have to mess with blogging or websites or releasing your own products if you don't want to or you aren't ready for that yet. You can focus on writing emails and promoting things as an affiliate.

But, when you are ready, adding the other passive income streams can help you grow your list on autopilot.

For example, I highly recommend you include an enticing freebie offer in each of the Kindle books you publish.

You can put a link to an opt-in form or squeeze page in the front matter and back matter of your published Kindle books. Give something away for free that will really entice Kindle readers. Once you have them on your list, you can talk about new books you release on Kindle as well as the other products you recommend.

You can also build your list via info-products you've released. You can set it up so that every time someone buys your product, they are added to your list. This is an autopilot way to grow your list when you have affiliates promoting for you.

When a buyer is added to your list, you benefit greatly—it's even better than getting someone on your list that downloaded your freebie. They've bought from you before, so they are much more likely to buy from you again.

Blogging is another nice way to grow your list. Hopefully, if you run a blog, you focus on growing your audience and really getting to know your audience. You should include opt-in forms on every page of your blog. Entice people to sign up so they can get the latest news and information and consider giving them a freebie. You can then email them and push them to your other offers as well.

Everything you do online should be tied to getting emails on your list. Your list is a fantastic passive income stream that is irreplaceable. Good, consistent autoresponder emails help build relationships and make sales for you. Email list marketers have it made!

Give people every opportunity to sign up for your list. The more opt-in boxes and squeeze pages you have, the better.

Passive Income Stream #5: Product Creation

Creating info products for the web is a fantastic passive income stream. People have problems they are desperate to have solved—and they are willing to pay for it. You can create products, like the one you're reading right now, that help serve their needs.

The info products you create can be PDF, video, audio, software, or a combination of multiples of the above. These are essentially digital courses that help people solve a problem or fulfill a passion they have.

You're reading an info product right now. If you set up a network of info products and allow affiliates to promote them for you, you can earn an incredible income.

Info products generally sell for a lot more than standard ebooks. That's often because they contain more specialized information or are released in niches that can handle a higher price tag. In many cases, info products are more like college textbooks then standard ebooks, therefore requiring a higher price tag. The perceived value of things like video and audio tends to be higher as well.

Consider some of the info products you've purchased in the past. You may have purchased an info product related to a health problem of yours. You may have purchased many of the info products related to building a better business. Consider why you were willing to pay a premium for this kind of information and what the product creator included to help you feel like the purchase was worth it.

In cases where you feverishly and excitedly clicked on the buy button, consider why that was. Info products tend to be sold via sales pages that really hit on your emotions and needs. Business-to-business products and weight-loss products are especially sold this way.

What You Need

You have to choose a great niche. Find a need and fulfill that need and you can make great sales with your info products. It's important to get affiliates on board, and to give them a percentage of the sales they refer. You can also sell to your own audience, which is where the email list that I've recommended that you build comes in.

Some of the information products you sell might be lower end and lower-priced and other information products you sell might be higher end and higher-priced.

The overall focus is that you're solving a problem and providing a solution to that problem.

You can release your info product via a well-written PDF file. Or, you can create a PowerPoint or use screencast software to create a video. There are certain subjects that are better served by video. There are still other subjects that are better served by audio. In that case, you can use something like Audacity to create your audio file.

These info products can be part of a larger sales funnel. You can get people on your list using your freebie and squeeze page. You can then upsell them to a paid info product via a sales page. Consider what you would like your sales funnel to look like and get one set up.

Get a ton of high-quality info products out there with a ton of affiliates promoting them—it's a wonderful way to quickly build a massive passive income stream.

The Five Steps You Should Take

Step one:

The first step, of course, is finding a great niche. Not every niche out there has a large number of people interested in buying info products. As I mentioned already, business-to-business consumers are very used to buying info products like this one. There are certainly other niches you can find if you're not interested in this niche.

Browse ClickBank.com to find other niches that have an active buying audience for info products. You can also get ideas from Nanacast.com and JVZoo.com.

Next, start to outline the product you're going to release. If you don't enjoy writing, then you can absolutely create a video or audio course. You can also combine written reports and ebooks with visuals like mind maps and videos. The more value you add for the buyer, the better.

To create a complete sales funnel, create front end and back end products. Find bonuses to further entice people to buy. You might include a report or ebook on the front end and then upsell people to personalized help and coaching. Or, you might consider creating a membership site or a course to upsell people to.

Emulate marketers you admire to get a grip on what you want your info product sales funnel to look like.

Step two:

Now it's time to do the actual work of creating your front end and back end products (or just a front end product, if you want to start small). Get your product written or created and polish it off so it's as professional as possible.

If you're stuck for ideas, look for specific questions people in your niche ask on forums. See what they are chatting about on social media. Look at the other products that are available. Browse related books on Amazon.

Find a unique twist for your product—make it different from everything else out there, in some way.

Don't feel like you have to create a masterpiece the first time around. Your ebook could be just 5,000-10,000 words. Find one problem people are willing to pay good money to solve and offer them a single, highly workable solution. Rinse and repeat.

Step three:

Next, it's time to set up the technical details. You need to write and format a sales page. Visit sales pages you've bought from yourself to get an idea of what this should look like. You may want to consider hiring a copywriter to maximize conversions. Otherwise, learn how to write high converting copy yourself.

You also need to figure out product delivery. You can use services like JVZoo or Nanacast to help you deliver your products and get sales and affiliates.

One of the main things you focus on is getting affiliates on board. Services like JVZoo make that easy. The more affiliates you have, the better. They can tap into their existing lists and networks to make sales. That's how you make sales and grow your list even when you're brand new!

Since you'll have (hopefully) tied all of your product sales to your list, all of their buyers will get added to your list so you can sell to them again and again. This is amazing—imagine how many more sales you'll get when you release your next product.

Please don't neglect to add buyers to your list – that's a huge mistake and you'll be leaving a lot of money on the table.

Step four:

Focus on getting more affiliates on board and advertise your sales page. Affiliates will do a lot for you. Make sure you treat your affiliates right and give them materials that will help them sell so they'll advertise your products over and over again.

You might also consider running paid ads to sell your product. You can run ads on networks like Google Adwords, Bing, Facebook, and more. Paid ads can help you figure out right away if your sales page is going to convert well or not—you won't have to wait for organic traffic.

Remember to send paid traffic to a squeeze page first. Get people on your list and start that relationship and it will be so much easier for you to make sales. You'll get a lot more for your advertising dollar if you direct to a squeeze page first and then upsell those who take the freebie bait.

Hopefully, you're also working on establishing a presence on social media. You really want the people of your niche to know, like, and trust you. You want them to hang on your every word and wait anxiously until you release your next product. That's the goal anyway.

Step five:

Once you have one product up and selling, it's time to work on your next product. Don't stop at just one! Your goal is to release many products over time. If you have many products out there that are converting well and that affiliates are pushing for you, you can earn on autopilot.

Get a lot of affiliates and grow your list. Get your list excited about the products you're going to release in the future.

Run special contests that will get affiliates excited about promoting for you. Be very generous with your affiliate commissions. It can also help if you get affiliates to sign up for a separate affiliate list so that you can tell them about upcoming launches.

Remind them to promote for you more than once. The squeaky wheel gets the grease. You want to have a great relationship with your affiliates so make sure you treat them well.

Rinse and repeat your success. Release products and grow your list. Get more affiliates on board. Promote your list. Do everything you can to grow your list, get more affiliates to promote for you, advertise your sales pages, and make money on autopilot.

Tying This Together with Other Passive Income Streams

Selling info products and building a list in this way will help you with your other passive income streams as well. For instance, you can advertise to your info product customers that you are going to release a book on Kindle.

You can advertise to your following when you write a new blog post or create a new page or group on social media. It all works hand in hand.

We haven't talked about continuity programs or membership sites in detail yet, but you absolutely can tie that passive income stream together with your info product income stream.

Your continuity program can be a fantastic upsell in your funnel. Or, depending on how you structure it, it can be a lead-in to your higher end products.

Passive Income Stream #6: Continuity Programs

Continuity programs are an extremely smart passive income business model for you. Essentially, these are membership sites or membership offers of some kind. People will join your offer, expecting to be re-billed every month (or at whatever interval you've advertised).

It's so much easier to get the same customer to pay you again and again then it is to get a brand new customer. This is especially true when the process is automated.

If someone signs up for your continuity program or membership site and likes it, they are likely to stick around. The re-bill happens on autopilot so the money comes out of their bank account or PayPal account without them having to take further action. This is fantastic news for you. You can easily build up a passive income stream if you run a great membership program.

PayPal makes it easy to set up payments in this way. JVZoo and other programs offer an easy way to connect payments with membership software.

There are also a variety of membership site plug-ins available for platforms like WordPress. Just find the membership site software that suits your needs.

Brainstorm a hot topic people will pay you monthly to learn more about. Figure out ways you can over-deliver on content every month.

You could run a paid continuity forum. You could run a continuity program where people get new info products every month. You could run a coaching continuity program. You could have software that rebills customers on a regular basis to continue to receive updates and upgrades.

There really isn't a limit to the things you can do with a continuity program. Make it so enticing and exciting that people will sign up without hesitation.

What You Need

What you need for this is similar to what you need to sell info products. You need a website with an enticing sales page that will get people to sign up for your continuity offer.

You also need membership software that handles who's paid and who gets access and who doesn't. The best membership software will also help you deliver content at certain intervals and to certain people. You could have free membership levels and paid membership levels.

PayPal is a very popular option for continuity programs. PayPal integrates with some of the most popular WordPress membership plug-ins.

Above all, you'll need great content. If people are going to be paying monthly for your membership site, then you should over-deliver with what you offer them.

I give my Earn 1K A Day members a ton of products I've purchased rights to. I also give them most of my own products I release online, including many of the higher-end ones. Not to mention the personalized, high-level help they get whenever they have a question.

Many people join membership sites like Earn 1K A Day because they get so much more value, a family-like community, and so much more interaction.

The Five Steps You Should Take

Step one:

First, research to find successful membership sites in your niche. Figure out what makes those continuity programs unique and brainstorm your own great ideas. Note what makes a successful membership site and what breaks an unsuccessful membership site.

Step two:

Now it's time to get the technical details figured out. Do some digging to figure out which membership site solution you want to use. In many cases, you can use PayPal to collect your payments (go with what's familiar and easy to you). Figure how you're going to deliver content and other odds and ends. Tools like WishList Member and WP MemberChamp can help you figure it all out.

Step three:

Now, fill your membership site to the brim with great content that goes beyond what people expect.

Develop great sales materials and get affiliates on board to get people to sign up for your continuity program. Make it very clear that you have the best membership site in your niche.

Brainstorm ways you can make your membership site stand above everyone else's.

Step four:

Once you have a membership site set up and your sales page is ready to go, it's time to start advertising. You might want to first advertise to your list before you go for a bigger launch with affiliates.

This is especially a good thing if you have a forum or active membership component, because you'll get the most avid followers chatting away first. Busy membership forums are more enticing and keep people around better than dead ones.

You can start to run paid traffic to your membership site. You may want to first direct people to a squeeze page where they can receive something for free. Then, either as an upsell or in subsequent messages, you can present the sales page for your membership site.

As always, it's important to get affiliates on board. Affiliates will love that you're starting a membership site because they'll get a cut of the profits every single month. When you're trying to recruit affiliates, make it clear that they will receive money this month and for every month their buyer remains a paid member.

Step five:

As you have new members signing up and you're generating a buzz in your marketplace, continue adding new content to boost value. Make it such a good value that people won't want to ever leave.

Consider the community aspect. Often, people join membership sites not intending to stick around. But they come to love the community and want to stick around because they've made friends and that's where their friends are.

They'll also stick around if you're a helpful and active part of your own membership. They'll want to learn from you and interact with you and your membership site is one of the best ways to do that.

Tying This Together with Other Passive Income Streams

This can work the other way as well. You can maintain a low priced membership site and upsell people to higher end info products and coaching. I personally like to include my info products as part of the membership in Earn 1K A Day. Test and track and see what will work for you.

You can advertise your membership site in your info products. You can talk a lot about it on your blog and everywhere you are online. You can tell your list about it frequently. You can entice additional JV partners and affiliates to promote for you.

Remember that people aren't likely to join the very first time they hear about your site. But, because you are running a membership site for the long-term, and people keep running into it, they will be much more likely to join. When they do, that's more passive income for you. It will snowball from there.

Be A Self-Starter For Incredible Passive Income

No matter which passive income stream you choose to start with, it's important that you are a self-starter. Don't expect to just read about these business models and think they'll work for you without any effort.

You have to work for this. Work hard and then you can live the passive income lifestyle. Work hard up front and then do the maintenance along the way. You can dramatically cut down on your overall work hours and dramatically boost your income.

Remember that if you have a question about any of the above income streams or any of the steps, you have to stop at nothing to find the answer. Google it or YouTube it.

Look to those who have set up these passive income streams successfully. If you're feeling stuck in any way, you can often get inspired by looking at what others have done.

Join together with a group of people who are focused on the same income stream. Work together to get things done.

People who are destined to succeed stop at nothing. They don't let anything stand in their way.

People who are destined to fail time and time again always come up with excuses as to why they can't do something. They'll say,

"Oh you left this step out so I can't do it" or, "You left that step out so I can't possibly succeed."

It's all a matter of mindset. A self-starter has a mindset of success and abundance and finds the answer.

Someone who is destined to fail remains negative and always finds a reason why he or she can't do it.

But you're not like that – you can do it and you will do it. You're going to choose the passive income stream that appeals to you the most. You're going to start with it and push through until you are successful, and I just know that you're going to combine more than one passive income stream together for your ultimate benefit.

Tie Your Income Streams Together

Once you have one passive income stream up and running, it's time to combine it with another one.

Tie your income streams together.

If you focus on list building and creating info products, for example, you've got a solid, combined business that can produce for you on autopilot.

If you combine your blog with Kindle marketing, you have two passive income streams that can work for you on autopilot.

You just have to figure out your roadmap. Which business models are you going to use to change your life? Make a plan for yourself, right here and right now. What are you going to start with? What are you going to do after you have that one up and running?

Normally the second one will come easier to you than the first, because some of the steps (for example determining what your niche will be) only needs to be done once.

Set your goals and figure out which passive income streams will allow you to achieve those goals. Build passive income stream on top of passive income stream, ideally in the same niche.

People shouldn't be able to search for products or information on topics related to your niche without stumbling upon you and the opportunity to buy from you.

Get those buy buttons up on the web.

Stay on Top of Your Passive Income Streams

I wish I could say that these were all 100% set it and forget it business models. Unfortunately, that just doesn't exist. You have to do the work to get these income streams up and running.

The good news is, that once you have one passive income stream up and running, it won't take nearly as much work to profit from it month after month than it took for the first month.

Stay on top of them and check in every once in a while so the income doesn't dwindle away.

In the meantime, enjoy yourself. Enjoy your passive income and the ability to rest and relax and live the life you want to live.

Keep releasing new Kindle books and info products. Keep adding value to your membership site and working to get more affiliates on board. Keep adding to your blog or website. Keep building your list like crazy.

Yes, you can sip piña coladas on the beach and still earn an income, if you want to.

You just have to check in on that income every once in a while. Once you get things up and running, it really can be just a few hours a day or week that you spend on your business, depending on your business model.

Maybe you choose to work part time and still earn a full-time income. That's absolutely possible once you've worked hard to get multiple passive income streams set up in the first place.

You probably won't earn a six-figure income by next week. But you could earn that this year if you stack passive income stream on top of passive income stream.

The work you do in one hour doesn't have to translate into what you earn per hour. The hour of work you do today can pay off for you for the rest of your life. You have to work hard now and you have to want this badly enough to follow through no matter what.

Managing Your Income Streams

Remember that the beginning of this is the hardest part. You're going to use some elbow grease upfront so you can reap the rewards later on. If you can push through and get each passive income stream up and running, then you can and will be successful.

Always be looking to tweak your strategy. Automate and outsource where you can. There may be certain things you love to do in your business and other things you don't love to do in your business. Don't just neglect these things, find other ways to do them

Once you have these passive income streams up and running, you can develop a schedule that will work for you. You can live the life of your dreams on your own terms as long as you plan ahead, set your goals, and focus on your Reason Why.

It's time you made this a reality. You don't have to struggle anymore. You don't have to go another day without having your own passive income streams set up all over the web.

I want you to stack success upon success. Choose the business model you're going to start with. Make sure you're focused on creating a brand people will come to love in your niche. Then, add another passive income stream. Rinse and repeat.

Soon enough, you'll become one of the people others admire so much because you're so successful. They'll think you have superpowers because you're earning a full-time income with passive income streams all over the web.

That's something to celebrate.

That's something to pat yourself on the back about. Congratulations – you're about to change your own life, starting this very minute.

Now, without further delay, go out there and do it!

www.ingramcontent.com/pod-product-compliance
Lightning Source LLC
Chambersburg PA
CBHW060843220526
45466CB00003B/1218